TIP FOR BETTER BRIDGE

Bernard Magee

BATSFORD

First published 2005

© Bernard Magee 2005

The right of Bernard Magee to be identified as Author of this work has been asserted by him in accordance with the Copyright, Designs and Patents Act 1988.

ISBN 0 7134 8992 8

A CIP catalogue record for this book is available from the British Library.

Typeset in the U.K. by Ruth Edmondson
Printed in the U.K. by Creative Print & Design, Ebbw Vale, Wales

for the publishers

B T Batsford, The Chrysalis Building, Bramley Road, London W10 6SP

An imprint of **Chrysalis** Books Group plc

Distributed in the United States and Canada by Sterling Publishing Co., 387 Park Avenue South, New York, NY 10016, USA

Editor: Elena Jeronimidis

Always consider bidding spades if you can

When the points are evenly distributed it is usually the side with spades that wins the bidding battle, because they are the highest-[ran]king suit. Spades create greater problems: a 1♠ overcall followed by [a r]aise to 2♠ can be very obstructive, and make your opponents' [auct]ion so much more difficult. Furthermore, if you are contemplating [a sac]rifice bid, then with a spade fit you can bid the suit at the same [level] as the opponents' game.

[All] of this should persuade you that making borderline calls with the [spade] suit is worthwhile. An important example is when considering [wheth]er to open the bidding fourth in hand, after three passes. [Typica]lly if you have a close decision with between 10 and 12 points, [the] points are likely to be split relatively evenly between the two [and] therefore the side with the spade suit is likely to win the [bidding]. What this means is that you should take the number of spades [in your] hand into account when making your decision; add the [number o]f spades to your points, and if the total comes to fifteen then [open the bid].

[Here is a] deal that illustrates the obstructive power of spade bids:

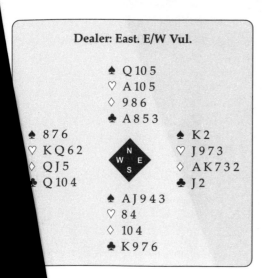

Dealer: East. E/W Vul.

```
                ♠ Q 10 5
                ♡ A 10 5
                ♢ 9 8 6
                ♣ A 8 5 3
    ♠ 8 7 6                  ♠ K 2
    ♡ K Q 6 2      N         ♡ J 9 7 3
    ♢ Q J 5      W   E       ♢ A K 7 3 2
    ♣ Q 10 4       S         ♣ J 2
                ♠ A J 9 4 3
                ♡ 8 4
                ♢ 10 4
                ♣ K 9 7 6
```

Contents

Bidding Tips

Declarer-play Tips

Defence Tips

General Tips

BIDDING TI

Auction 1

West	North	East	South
		1◊	Pass
1♡	Pass	2♡	All Pass

Auction 2

West	North	East	South
		1◊	1♠
Dbl	2♠	3♡	Pass
4♡	All Pass		

As South, you have a relatively weak hand, but with five spades you should always contemplate an overcall: the vulnerability is in your favour (East-West are vulnerable, you are not); a spade will probably make a reasonable lead; and your bid may well make life difficult for your opponents – these should be enough reasons to propel you into the auction.

In Auction 1, with no interference, East-West easily found their fit and were able to evaluate their hands accurately.

In Auction 2, West used a negative double to show four hearts, but when his partner bid 3♡ he thought he was worth a raise to game with 10 points and a good fit with both hearts and diamonds. The accuracy of the auction has disappeared; the partnership did well enough to find their heart fit, but they were not sure of each other's strength and thus went overboard.

4♡ would actually go two off. North-South can make nine tricks in spades, but +200 is even better than that!

Because of the power of the spade suit, you should tend to stretch your 1♠ overcalls more than any other; your partner, of course, should be doing the same thing and both of you need to take this into account. When you are contemplating how high to bid opposite a spade overcall, remember that your partner might have stretched!

Bid more aggressively when non-vulnerable

TIP 2

Non-vulnerable undertricks just cost 50 points each, so if you avoid being doubled, two down will often get you a great score: -100 leaves you better off than most of the part-scores that your opponents could make, -110 for 2♡ or 2♠ for example.

It is very important to get into the habit of competing for the part-score aggressively, especially when the auction dies at the two level.

Here you are South with nobody vulnerable:

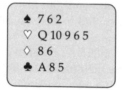

♠ 7 6 2
♡ Q 10 9 6 5
♢ 8 6
♣ A 8 5

The auction starts:

West	North	East	South
		1♢	Pass
1♠	Pass	2♣	Pass
2♢	Pass	Pass	?

With just 6 points, surely you cannot consider a call, you might think. But *where* are all the points?

If the opponents cannot make game, partner must have at least 11 or 12 points; he hasn't made a bid because he is too flat, which means it is up to you to bid for him! Since you passed over 1♢, it will be clear that you are not very strong. It is almost always wrong to sell out to your opponents in two-of-a-minor if they appear to have found a moderate fit.

East-West are likely to have at least a seven-card fit, if not an eight-card fit, in diamonds, and you would expect them to make their contract for a score of 90, or more likely score an overtrick for 110. You can clearly out-score this if you make 2♡, but perhaps more importantly you out-score it if you go one down – and might even out-score it if you go two off. Bearing this in mind, I hope you can see that the risks are not so high in bidding 2♡. Every so often something might go wrong, but nine out of ten times you will obtain a better score by competing.

So you bid 2♡ and it wins the auction. The full deal is:

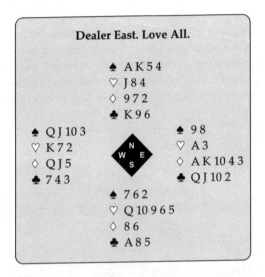

Dealer East. Love All.

	♠ A K 5 4	
	♡ J 8 4	
	◇ 9 7 2	
	♣ K 9 6	
♠ Q J 10 3		♠ 9 8
♡ K 7 2		♡ A 3
◇ Q J 5		◇ A K 10 4 3
♣ 7 4 3		♣ Q J 10 2
	♠ 7 6 2	
	♡ Q 10 9 6 5	
	◇ 8 6	
	♣ A 8 5	

As you can see; with your hands being so flat you will go one off in 2♡, but -50 is a triumph with East-West being able to score an easy 110. As predicted, your partner had a healthy collection of points but was so flat he was unable to bid. Quite often in these competitive deals, it is the hand with the distribution, rather than the points, that has to do the bidding.

How aggressive you can be at the two and three levels depends on how often you are likely to get doubled; generally too few club players double low-level part-scores, and therefore aggressive bidders can get away with murder. Use this to your advantage: compete more aggressively when you are non-vulnerable and you will be surprised by the number of good results you can gain by going one or two off.

Always double when the opponents steal your deal

TIP 3

When you have enough strength for game, do not let your opponents outbid you without punishing them with a double. On many occasions your opponents may have bid well and found a good sacrifice, but you still need to obtain as many points as you can.

Here you are South, vulnerable against non-vulnerable opposition:

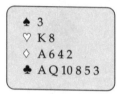

♠ 3
♡ K 8
♢ A 6 4 2
♣ A Q 10 8 5 3

The bidding starts:

West	North	East	South
	1♡	1♠	2♣
4♠	Pass	Pass	?

What are you going to call?

Don't you just hate it when your opponents do this to you? Barrage bidding is very difficult to deal with. West's bid is an excellent one, putting the maximum pressure on you. This is your deal; you decided that as soon as your partner opened the bidding: you have a good 13 points and he should have at least 12. You were planning to have a nice auction to the best game contract, but unfortunately that opportunity has been taken away from you. The one thing you must not do is pass because this is your deal and you cannot let the other side steal it away from you without at least getting a little compensation.

Bidding on to the five level would be guesswork, so perhaps your best option is simply to double. Your opponents might make their contract one out of ten times, but that should not worry you – keep on doubling them when they steal your deal!

What would you lead with the South hand above?

Ask yourself how East-West are going to make their tricks. The answer must be by trumping, so a trump lead has to be the right move; this is usually a good way to start the defence against weak sacrifice bidding, although it doesn't make a difference on this deal. The full layout is:

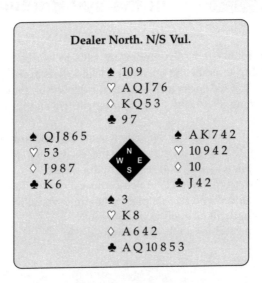

Dealer North. N/S Vul.

	♠ 10 9	
	♡ A Q J 7 6	
	◇ K Q 5 3	
	♣ 9 7	
♠ Q J 8 6 5		♠ A K 7 4 2
♡ 5 3		♡ 10 9 4 2
◇ J 9 8 7		◇ 10
♣ K 6		♣ J 4 2
	♠ 3	
	♡ K 8	
	◇ A 6 4 2	
	♣ A Q 10 8 5 3	

East-West have bid very aggressively, but at favourable vulnerability it often works. They have done tremendously well and even with your double you can only collect 100 points for one off. However, that is 50 more points than for 4♠ undoubled. Furthermore, you did well to take your 100 points because you would have struggled to make any contract at the five level. The five level is often difficult in auctions like these, because your opponents have advertised distributional hands, so some of the side suits are likely to break badly.

Do not let your opponents steal your deals without at least an element of pay-back: double them!

A take-out double shows shortage in the suit doubled

Take-out doubles are very important calls in bridge: they allow a partnership to enter the auction and find their best fit, especially when a strong hand lacks a five-card suit. However, they do carry a specific meaning: *they show shortage in the suit bid and support for all of the unbid suits.*

Shortage in the bid suit is the key element: the take-out double tells your partner that you do not want the deal to be played in the opponents' suit, and asks him to bid anything else.

With a very strong hand (19+) you can use a double with any shape but if it is balanced you have a plan: you aim to rebid in no-trumps – the extra strength allows you to do this safely.

This hand is perfect for a take-out double of 1♠:

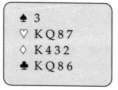

♠ 3
♡ K Q 8 7
◇ K 4 3 2
♣ K Q 8 6

However, the situation would be different over a 1♣ opener. Now the shape is not suitable for a take-out double and since overcalls show five-card suits you would have to pass.

Why can you not just double to show an opening hand?

Because then partner cannot judge what to do in response, whereas if he knows that you want to play in the other suits he can bid accordingly. For example:

♠ 3		♠ 876	
♡ KQ87		♡ AJ10 3	
◇ K432		◇ 7	
♣ KQ86		♣ AJ952	

West	North	East	South
			1♠
Dbl	Pass	2♠¹	Pass
3♣	Pass	3♡	Pass
4♡	All Pass		

¹Showing strength

West makes a take-out double over South's 1♠ opening and East can get excited. With a fit for two of the unbid suits, a singleton and his weakness opposite shortage in his partner's hand, East has enough for a game contract. He bids the opponent's suit to show his strength; West bids his lowest suit; although East likes clubs, he would prefer it if they had a fit in a major, so he tries 3♡ which West then raises to game.

(Bidding the opponents' suit is an important part of competitive bidding; it is not natural: it just shows strength and demands that partner bid again.)

A great auction to a very good game, but note that East can only evaluate his hand so aggressively if he can be confident of his partner's hand. The double fit (his partner has shown support for all the unbid suits) and, perhaps most importantly, East's horrible holding in spades (8-7-6) are key: East needs to be confident that his spade losers can be dealt with and indeed, if his partner has shortage in spades, they can be ruffed.

Change West's hand and you can see that East's evaluation does not work so well:

♠ K93		♠ 876	
♡ KQ87		♡ AJ10 3	
◇ K43		◇ 7	
♣ Q86		♣ AJ952	

The same 23 points, but West is unable to deal with East's spade weakness, nor is there such a pronounced double fit. East-West are only likely to manage nine tricks.

"Borrow" a king to keep the auction open

Unless a hand is a complete misfit, then with a relatively equal split of points both sides should be able to compete for the part-score. Therefore, if your opponents settle in a fit at the two level, something is wrong: you should be competing, so think hard before you pass.

Look at this example. You, as South, hold:

♠ 8
♡ A 9 5 2
♢ Q 7 6 5
♣ Q J 9 8

Nobody is vulnerable and the auction starts:

West	North	East	South
		1♠	Pass
2♠	Pass	Pass	?

You passed on the first round because with just 9 points you were not strong enough to make a bid, but things have changed somewhat. Your opponents seem to have a fit and yet they have stopped at the two level. Before you pass this out, you need seriously to contemplate making a call. Where are all the points?

Your partner must have some strength because otherwise the opponents would surely have bid to game. Bearing this in mind, you should "borrow" a king from your partner and then see if you would make a call; if the answer is yes, then make the call!

If I added the ♢K to your hand, would you not make a take-out double? Well, that is exactly what you should do.

There are two reasons for this: firstly, you might be able to make a contract at the three level and secondly, even if you cannot make a contract, by going down in your contract you will get a better score than letting the other side make their 2♠ contract.

Here is the full deal:

Tips for Better Bridge

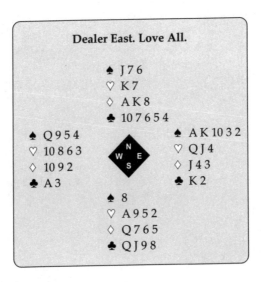

Dealer East. Love All.

```
              ♠ J 7 6
              ♡ K 7
              ◊ A K 8
              ♣ 10 7 6 5 4
♠ Q 9 5 4                    ♠ A K 10 3 2
♡ 10 8 6 3        N          ♡ Q J 4
◊ 10 9 2      W     E        ◊ J 4 3
♣ A 3            S           ♣ K 2
              ♠ 8
              ♡ A 9 5 2
              ◊ Q 7 6 5
              ♣ Q J 9 8
```

In response to your take-out double North would bid 3♣, forcing East-West on to 3♠. You can actually make 4♣ on the deal, but more importantly 3♠ is certain to be defeated, most likely by just one trick – although if you could see through the backs of the cards you could get a heart ruff for two off and 200 points.

You can see how important competing for the part-score can be: if you allow East-West to make 2♠ that would be -110, whilst you could be making +130. That is a 240 point difference – which is surely worth fighting for.

Whenever your opponents stop at the two level you need to ask yourself where all the points are. What is important to remember is that bidding on balanced hands after your opponents have opened is very difficult; with no suit to show, nor perhaps the strength to overcall 1NT, nor shortage in their bid suit, you can be stuck with as many as 14 or 15 points. However, there is no need to worry too much, for you should be confident that if the bidding dies out, your partner will be aware of your predicament and borrow one of your kings to try to make a bid himself. Most often it is the player who is short in the opponents' suit who needs to make the call, because he will be able to make a take-out double.

The right conditions for such bids are much more frequent than you might think. Here is an example where only one opponent manages a bid:

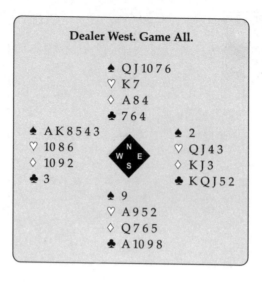

Dealer West. Game All.

```
                    ♠ Q J 10 7 6
                    ♡ K 7
                    ◇ A 8 4
                    ♣ 7 6 4
  ♠ A K 8 5 4 3                    ♠ 2
  ♡ 10 8 6          N               ♡ Q J 4 3
  ◇ 10 9 2       W     E            ◇ K J 3
  ♣ 3              S                ♣ K Q J 5 2
                    ♠ 9
                    ♡ A 9 5 2
                    ◇ Q 7 6 5
                    ♣ A 10 9 8
```

West	North	East	South
2♠¹	Pass	Pass	Dbl
All Pass			

¹Weak Two bid: 6-10 points and a six-card suit

West opens a Weak Two in spades and North keeps quiet – he cannot double because that would be asking you to take-out. East also passes and it is your turn. Once again you should consider carefully before passing: your opponents have shown no great strength in the auction (West's bid has shown 6-10 points); you should be asking yourself where all the points are. Once again you should assume that some are in your partner's hand and therefore you should take one of his kings and see if you would make a call.

Of course, adding a king to your hand makes double a very desirable call: you would like to play in any suit other than spades. The beauty of this particular double is that it brings a great big smile to your partner's face: he is very happy to play in spades and so passes. You get a little shock because you are worried partner has forgotten the system, but no need to worry – his trumps make three tricks to go with the four top tricks you have between you, and then the ◇Q might score too! 2♠ doubled two off is 500 points (three off would be worth 800!).

There are so many reasons to reopen auctions at low levels that this tip needs to be taken seriously. Notice, however, that each of the hands shown are short in the opponents' suit. That is a key point: aggressive re-opening works best when you are short in the opponents' suit.

Tips for Better Bridge

After a penalty double, don't let the opponents escape

Once you have made a penalty double, your side is suggesting that it is the boss; you should therefore behave that way and punish your opponents! Quite often after you have doubled them a first time, they will try to escape; do not let them escape unless you have to – keep doubling them if you have length in their suit.

You open 1♡ with the following hand:

> ♠ 7 3
> ♡ A K 9 5 2
> ◇ 4 2
> ♣ A J 6 5

The auction continues as below:

West	North	East	South
			1♡
1NT	Dbl	2♣	?

What do you bid now?

North's double of West's 1NT overcall is straightforward – it simply says that our side has the majority of the points and therefore we would expect to take 1NT down. What does East's 2♣ mean?

After the double, it is natural: he is trying to escape from 1NT; he has length in clubs but very few points. Do not let the opponents run away – if you have length you can double them again.

You do indeed have four clubs and so should double.

Had you not had length you would not have doubled, because you need both high-card-point strength and good trumps to double at low levels.

Turn over to see the full deal:

Dealer South. Game All.

```
                    ♠ J 8 6 5
                    ♡ 10 3
                    ◇ A J 9 8 6
                    ♣ K Q
    ♠ A K Q                         ♠ 10 9 4 2
    ♡ Q J 8 6          N            ♡ 7 4
    ◇ K Q 5 3      W       E        ◇ 10 7
    ♣ 7 2              S            ♣ 10 9 8 4 3
                    ♠ 7 3
                    ♡ A K 9 5 2
                    ◇ 4 2
                    ♣ A J 6 5
```

West	North	East	South
			1♡
1NT	Dbl	2♣	Dbl
All Pass			

As you can see there are four top trumps, ♡A-K and ◇A available in defence for an easy two off and +500 – there are also chances for an eighth defensive trick to rub in the message!

The most common situation for this tip is when a 1NT opening is doubled; the opponents will frequently try to wriggle out of their predicament. Try not to let them run away; continue doubling unless you have reason to think they have a fit. Too often, after East's 2♣ bid (in the example above), South will fail to double and East-West will escape their punishment.

Halve the value
of a singleton honour
when opening

A singleton ace is always worth its full 4 points, but the value of any other singleton honour is dubious as they might lose to a higher card: a singleton king could fall under your opponents' ace and therefore be worthless, but then your partner could hold the ace or the queen of the suit and give your king back its strength. As the auction progresses you will get a fair idea of how strong or not your singleton honour might be, but as opening bidder you have to assess its worth. My advice is to count half the points for any singleton honour; this gives a fair value for its worth.

Note that when opening the bidding you should not add on points for any shortage; this is because a singleton, for example, is only useful if you play in a suit contract – and until you find a fit, you do not know whether you are going to play in a suit.

Here is an example with you as dealer at Game All:

> ♠ K 7 5 4
> ♡ K
> ◇ Q J 6 2
> ♣ A 8 7 6

With 13 high-card points it looks like an obvious opening bid, but consider that 4-4-4-1 hands are not the most desirable of opening hands because they are difficult to bid. Furthermore, if your opponents' ♡A kills your king, then you are left with a ropy 10-count. Using my halving rule leaves you with an 11½ point total and therefore at best a borderline opening bid. Bearing in mind, as I mentioned above, that 4-4-4-1 hands are awkward to bid, I would highly recommend passing with this hand. Don't forget that you can come back into the auction later if appropriate: your first-round pass simply states that you do not feel your hand is worthy of an opening bid.

The complete deal is shown overleaf:

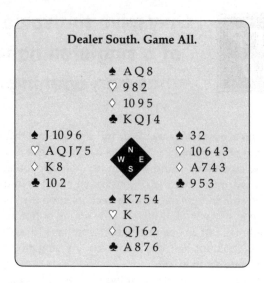

Dealer South. Game All.

> ♠ A Q 8
> ♡ 9 8 2
> ◊ 10 9 5
> ♣ K Q J 4

♠ J 10 9 6　　　　　　♠ 3 2
♡ A Q J 7 5　　　　　　♡ 10 6 4 3
◊ K 8　　　　　　　　　◊ A 7 4 3
♣ 10 2　　　　　　　　♣ 9 5 3

> ♠ K 7 5 4
> ♡ K
> ◊ Q J 6 2
> ♣ A 8 7 6

West	North	East	South
			Pass
1♡	Pass	2♡	Dbl
Pass	3♣	All Pass	

By passing at your first turn, you have limited your hand – and as the auction progresses you are glad you did so, because it seems that your ♡K is worthless. However, you are able to come into the auction on the second round; you have a maximum hand for your previous pass and you have the perfect shape: shortage in hearts and support for all the other suits, which means that you can compete the deal to the full. Your partner bids 3♣, but is not tempted to go any higher since you have limited your hand initially. If you had opened the bidding it might have been a different matter.

Only add length-points for a suit that might be useful

The reason for adding on points for length is because long suits can generate extra tricks – but some suits are better than others! Compare these two heart holdings:

(a) ♡ A K 8 7 6   **(b)** ♡ J 6 5 4 3

The holding in (a) is almost bound to feature in the play, and will more often than not be worth an extra trick. However, the holding in (b) is less useful: if we finish with hearts as trumps, then of course the fifth heart will be very handy but in no-trumps, or a different suit contract, this holding is very likely to be redundant.

When you have found a fit, you should add points for shortage and for useful length:

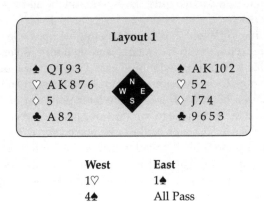

Layout 1

♠ QJ93		♠ AK102
♡ AK876		♡ 52
◇ 5		◇ J74
♣ A82		♣ 9653

West	East
1♡	1♠
4♠	All Pass

In this auction, West evaluates his hand using shortage and high-card points, but he also adds on a length point for his robust suit as it is likely to be valuable in the play. The Total Points come to 18 (including 3 points for a singleton for its ruffing value), so West goes for game.

Conversely (see next page):

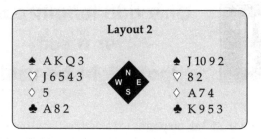

West	East
1♡	1♠
3♠	All Pass

In this second example, West does not add a point for length because his heart suit is so poor that it is unlikely to be of any worth during the play. With one fewer Total Point (17), West settles for a 3♠ response which East passes.

Let us see how the suit qualities affect the play, *assuming that the outstanding hearts break in the most likely fashion: 4-2.*

In Layout 1, declarer should be able to establish the heart suit with ease: he can win the ♡A-K, ruff a heart high, return to hand with a trump and ruff another heart high. Now his fifth heart will be a winner. He makes four trumps, two ruffs, ♡A-K, ♣A and the all-important fifth heart – ten tricks.

Contrast this to Layout 2: declarer has to give up the lead twice in hearts before trying to ruff two hearts, and then if he is very lucky he might be able to reach his winning heart. However, the defence can keep him to nine tricks by leading trumps from the start and then each time they win a heart trick, leaving declarer with just one trump in each hand and therefore able to ruff only one heart – not enough when the suit breaks 4-2. Declarer could have played for a 3-3 club break instead, but that too is likely to fail to generate a tenth trick.

Fully evaluating your hand is very important, but always remember how much more useful a strong and long suit is than a long but weak one.

Isolated honours are bad except in partner's suit

What do I mean by "isolated" honours, you might ask? Basically, honours that are by themselves in a suit which is consequently relatively weak. Honours always work better together, both for establishing tricks and finessing. Take a look at this hand:

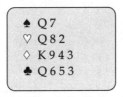

♠ Q 7
♡ Q 8 2
◇ K 9 4 3
♣ Q 6 5 3

This really is an ugly hand! With all the honours working by themselves, many of the 9 points will be wasted – probably half of the honours in this hand will die a swift death to an opponent's honour. Conversely, if you have 9 points in one suit, e.g. ♠ A-K-Q-3, you have three tricks.

Compare these two suits:

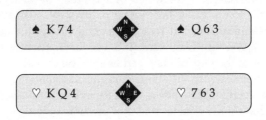

♠ K 7 4   ♠ Q 6 3

♡ K Q 4   ♡ 7 6 3

In spades you are only likely to make one trick because the defender with the ace should use it to kill one of your honours. However, in hearts you are able to lead up towards your honours together; can you see what happens if South has the ace? If he plays it you can play small, but if he ducks you can win the ♡K, cross back to the East hand and lead another heart putting South in a nasty predicament again. Basically you have a 50% chance of making two tricks in the suit when your honours are together.

Generally you should be wary of kings, queens and jacks that are on their own and if you have a borderline decision to make, this is one of the aspects of your hand that should sway your decision. However, you should also bear in mind that if your isolated honour is supported by partner's holding, it regains its strength, and thus an honour in you partner's suit can be very valuable, e.g.

	♠ K 7		♠ A J 10 8 2
	♡ K Q 10 7 6		♡ J 9 2
	◇ 8 5		◇ 9 6 4
	♣ A 9 8 2		♣ K 6

West	East
1♡	1♠
2♣	3♡
4♡	All Pass

Both players in this auction have added strength for honours in their partner's suit. The auction starts normally, both players showing their five-card majors and then West shows his second suit. East knows he has an eight-card fit in hearts, but how high should he go? With just 9 points he could be forgiven for staying low with 2♡, but this East is wiser than that: he adds a point for the strong and long suit (see Tip 8) and he also adds strength for his ♣K in his partner's suit. Over to West: 3♡ is an invitation to game, but West is pretty weak; isn't 12 high-card points a minimum? It is, but West has a good strong suit and his king of spades is just where West wants it to be – in his partner's suit.

Take a look at the two hands together and you can see how well the two kings combine with the strength in the other hand: they turn out to be worth a certain trick, just as good as an ace. 4♡ is a bold contract but it does have a reasonable chance of success.

Honours in your partner's suit are very valuable – always take into account your holdings in partner's suits when contemplating a close decision.

Use the jump shift sparingly

TIP 10

When you hold a strong hand opposite an opening bid, there is a temptation to try to tell partner the good news right away. However, there is no need for such urgency because partner has promised to make another bid, as long as you change the suit. Take your time; jumping a level in the bidding early on wastes precious space. Another major problem with making a jump shift response is that it detracts from the accuracy of the auction; we all know what our 1NT rebid, suit rebid or change of suits show, but these rebids are not so clear after a jump shift. Do rebids in no-trumps carry the same meaning or are they slightly negative? Is a new suit natural or trying for no-trumps? The clarity of the auction disappears quickly because we are not so used to auctions containing a jump. So try to avoid unnecessary jumps without good reason.

A jump shift should show 16 or more points and a good six-card suit. The bid is saying two things: (i) I seriously want to play in my suit, and (ii) I am strong enough to consider a slam.

You should certainly not consider a jump shift on a balanced hand.

Here are three East hands that are responding to a 1◇ opening bid:

Hand 1	**Hand 2**	**Hand 3**
♠ 3 2	♠ 3 2	♠ 3
♡ K Q J 9 8 4	♡ K Q J 9	♡ K Q J 9 2
◇ K 6	◇ K 8 6	◇ K 8
♣ A K 6	♣ A K 6 2	♣ A K 6 3 2

Hand 1 is an ideal hand for a jump-shift, with its 16 points and a robust heart suit. It is highly likely that hearts will make the best trump suit. Conversely, *Hand 2* is completely unsuitable for a jump shift, so start by responding 1♡ and allow your partner to describe his hand accurately. Finally, *Hand 3* is also unsuitable for a jump response because it is two-suited; you need the space to show both suits in order to try to find the best fit. Respond 1♡ and then bid your clubs.

```
          West
      ♠ 9 7
      ♡ A 3
      ◇ A Q 10 9 4
      ♣ Q J 8 7
```

This is a West hand for the East hands on page 25 (repeated below):

Hand 1	Hand 2	Hand 3
♠ 3 2	♠ 3 2	♠ 3
♡ K Q J 9 8 4	♡ K Q J 9	♡ K Q J 9 2
◇ K 6	◇ K 8 6	◇ K 8
♣ A K 6	♣ A K 6 2	♣ A K 6 3 2

Hand 1		Hand 2		Hand 3	
West	**East**	**West**	**East**	**West**	**East**
1◇	2♡	1◇	1♡	1◇	1♡
3♡	4♣	2♣	2♠	2♣	3♠
4◇	4♡	3◇	4♣	4♡	4NT
All Pass		5♣	All Pass	5♡	6♣
				All Pass	

On *Hand 1*, the heart suit is agreed right away and the partnership can use cue-bidding to discover no spade control and thus settle in 4♡.

By taking his time on *Hand 2*, East allows his side to find the best game and he tries for no-trumps by using a bid of 2♠, the fourth suit. When West bids 3◇, it is clear that there is no spade stop and therefore 3NT is out of the question, so East reverts to clubs and West raises to game.

By responding just 1♡ on *Hand 3*, East has given West the chance to show his second suit and thus uncover the excellent club fit. East now uses the extra space to have a thorough exploration. The jump to 3♠ is a "splinter bid" showing a singleton in spades and good club support. When West bids 4♡, showing the ♡A, East decides to risk using Blackwood. When West shows two aces, East can bid 6♣ with confidence.

The respective sequences are not so important, but the bidding space required to bid Hands 2 and 3 is essential in order to find the best denomination and the right level. Only take up bidding space if you have a suit that warrants it – the heart suit in *Hand 1* certainly does.

Consider passing
and letting
partner decide

The most common situation in which players struggle to keep quiet is when they have pre-empted, but then want to bid again. After you have pre-empted, you should let things be: you have done your work, and if you bid again you will only help the opponents.

It is equally important to keep quiet when, as the opening bidder, you have 17 points and partner passes. Say you hold this South hand:

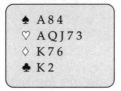

♠ A 8 4
♡ A Q J 7 3
♢ K 7 6
♣ K 2

At Game All, dealer South, the auction starts:

West	North	East	South
			1♡
1♠	Pass	1NT	?

You have a lovely hand – a good 17 points with a five-card suit. There is a temptation to bid again to tell partner about your high cards and your all-round strength, but does partner want to know? If he does, he will be strong enough to bid himself; it is more than likely that he holds very little since the opponents have both bid. His hand might be:

♠ 9 7 6 2
♡ 4
♢ J 8 4 2
♣ 10 9 4 3

Here partner certainly does not want to hear you bidding! However, if he holds a hand like the next one:

North can bid himself: by passing at his first turn he has shown a relatively weak hand, so a "late" 2◊ bid does not show great ambition, but it does allow the partnership to compete for the part-score.

Or North might hold:

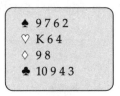

He did not support the hearts the first time because he did not want you to get excited, but with the bidding dying, North could bid 2♡ at his second turn, once again allowing your side to compete.

As you can see, South is not the player who can make an accurate decision, but North knows that South may want to make a bid and so as last bidder will try hard to help him. As we have seen in previous tips, *both* players of a partnership should try hard to make a bid when the auction dies at a low level, especially the last player to call.

Let's finish with a pre-empting example. You open 3♠, as South, with E/W Vul. After two passes, East bids 4♡; what do you call with the hand below?

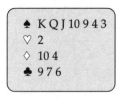

The answer, of course, is *pass*. Yes, you may be sure that 4♠ will be a good sacrifice against 4♡, and you may reason that you only need to make seven tricks (for -500) to compensate for the opponents' game and that you have six tricks, so if your partner has none, the other side should be in a slam! However, you are not thinking straight: your pre-empt has forced East to open the bidding at the four level; in fact, you have made him guess the final contract – how do you know it is going to make? The only person who can know that is your partner. He can decide whether game is on or not for your opponents and if he decides it is, then he can bid 4♠ himself. After all, you have told your partner what you have in your hand: 5-9 points and seven spades. The full deal is:

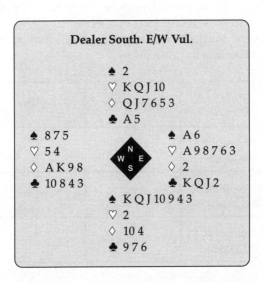

Dealer South. E/W Vul.

```
                    ♠ 2
                    ♡ K Q J 10
                    ◇ Q J 7 6 5 3
                    ♣ A 5
   ♠ 8 7 5                        ♠ A 6
   ♡ 5 4          N               ♡ A 9 8 7 6 3
   ◇ A K 9 8    W   E             ◇ 2
   ♣ 10 8 4 3     S               ♣ K Q J 2
                    ♠ K Q J 10 9 4 3
                    ♡ 2
                    ◇ 10 4
                    ♣ 9 7 6
```

Your opening bid has done its job: you have made East guess. His 4♡ bid is quite reasonable, but unfortunately there are four obvious losers, so he will go one off. North does not have too much difficulty working out that 4♡ is going off, so he doubles it – netting 200 points for your side. Had you rebid 4♠, your partner would not have been happy for two reasons: firstly you would probably lose 500 points, but secondly and most importantly you would have undermined partnership trust. A 4♠ rebid by South is tantamount to saying: "I do not trust my partner to do the right thing, so I will do it for him."

Passing can be very difficult, but giving partner the chance to be the "hero" instead of you can also be very rewarding.

**TIP
12**

You need two top honours for a second-seat pre-empt

A s you will see below it is important to be constructive when pre-empting in the second seat, so make sure you have two of the top three honours in the suit (ace, king or queen).

Most players overlook the importance of position when pre-empting, but consider the table below:

	Opponents	Partner
Pre-empting as dealer	2	1
Pre-empting in 2nd position	1	1
Pre-empting in 3rd position	1	0

A pre-emptive opening is a very descriptive bid, but its main aim is to disrupt the opponents' bidding. As dealer you are twice as likely to disrupt them rather than your partner; and in third seat, with two players having already passed, there is only one player left: an opponent. So in both these positions you can bid aggressively in the reasonable hope of disrupting your opponents' bidding and thus getting a better score - you do not need to be so strict about your suit strength. However, in the second seat you will be disrupting your partner half the time. This should certainly affect your style for two reasons: firstly, to have more constructive auctions and secondly, to keep your partner happy.

There is no need to make your pre-empts in second seat stronger but if you can promise a strong suit, partner will be able to make more accurate judgments when it turns out to be he who has the strong hand. The best way to go about this is to make sure that all second-seat pre-empts promise two of the top three honours in the suit. It is much easier to respond to a pre-empt if you stick to this tip.

Consider this example; you are East at Love All:

```
♠ 4                    ♠ A J 7 3
♡ 7 2          N       ♡ A 8 4
◇ 9 5 4      W   E     ◇ J 8 7 6
♣ A Q J 9 8 7 4  S     ♣ K 2
```

The auction starts:

West	North	East	South
			Pass
3♣	Pass	?	

With just 13 points opposite a weak opening bid, the temptation is to pass, but knowing that your partner holds two of the top three honours in clubs, you can count nine tricks in no-trumps and should bid 3NT. Without being sure of the solid clubs, you cannot be sure of nine tricks.

Here is another example:

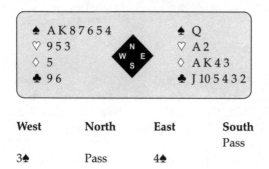

```
♠ A K 8 7 6 5 4        ♠ Q
♡ 9 5 3        N       ♡ A 2
◇ 5          W   E     ◇ A K 4 3
♣ 9 6          S       ♣ J 10 5 4 3 2
```

West	North	East	South
			Pass
3♠	Pass	4♠	

Once again, East holds one of the top three honours, and can rely on his partner holding the other two for his second-seat pre-empt. He reasons that on a normal 3-2 break in spades there will be ten tricks, so he raises to 4♠.

Put the brakes on
if you have
a misfit

Whenever you think your side has a misfit (no eight-card fit in any suit), then you should slow the auction down. Quite often, if you can stop at the two level you might just end up with a positive score, whilst most pairs will be playing in 3NT going two or three off. It will often pay to take a point or two off when evaluating your hand, since the difficulties involved in the play of misfitting hands can result in at least one trick fewer.

You are South, holding this rather nice collection at Game All:

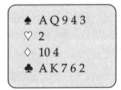

♠ A Q 9 4 3
♡ 2
♢ 10 4
♣ A K 7 6 2

The auction starts:

West	North	East	South
	1♡	Pass	1♠
Pass	2♢	Pass	?

What are you going to call?

Most players would blast out 3NT: "With thirteen points opposite an opening hand, surely game is on," they will think. However, with a big misfit, games are very difficult to make: invariably you will find that communications between the two hands will be a problem, so it will often pay to downgrade your hand just a little. 2NT seems an odd bid, but it would show about 11 points and invite game. Partner is only likely to pass if he has a minimum hand; with a good 13 or 14 points he will bid on. Thus with just 25 points you will miss the game and that is exactly your aim! Bear in mind that 25 points and a big misfit do not often translate into a making game unless you get some luck. Consider also that your partner may well have just 11 points if he has two five-card suits. If the full deal is as the one on the next page:

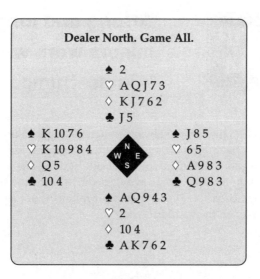

Dealer North. Game All.

```
                ♠ 2
                ♡ A Q J 7 3
                ◇ K J 7 6 2
                ♣ J 5
  ♠ K 10 7 6              ♠ J 8 5
  ♡ K 10 9 8 4     N      ♡ 6 5
  ◇ Q 5       W   E      ◇ A 9 8 3
  ♣ 10 4          S       ♣ Q 9 8 3
                ♠ A Q 9 4 3
                ♡ 2
                ◇ 10 4
                ♣ A K 7 6 2
```

On this layout North would pass 2NT and that is where you would play. The traveller will be filled with -200s, -300s and -400s for 3NT going off, but you have "saved" a trick and if you can manage just one or two off, you are likely to get a top score. Note that two out of three finesses are working in the above deal, but still with so little communication between the hands there is no chance of collecting nine tricks.

Playing teams of four it is difficult not to bid to game on such hands because the gains for bidding and making games are so high, but in a normal duplicate pairs, playing safe when you have a misfit can pay great dividends.

Strong and long minors work well in no-trumps

Try to get into the habit of always contemplating a no-trump contract when you have a good minor-suit fit, or simply a long and strong minor. It is a good habit to adopt, especially at duplicate pairs: making eleven tricks in a minor is always difficult, whilst nine tricks in no-trumps (with six tricks coming from your minor) is not so difficult.

For example, on the hand below:

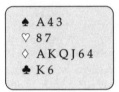

♠ A 4 3
♡ 8 7
◊ A K Q J 6 4
♣ K 6

You would open in diamonds of course (1◊), but you should be keeping no-trumps in mind as the auction develops.

However, the most common situation for minors to come good in no-trumps is when you hold support for your partner's minor suit and can therefore "see" the suit running.

You are South holding:

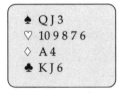

♠ Q J 3
♡ 10 9 8 7 6
◊ A 4
♣ K J 6

It is Game All and the auction starts:

West	North	East	South
1♠	2♣	2♠	?

Your partner has made a vulnerable two-level overcall, so he should surely have a reasonable six-card suit. Since you hold the ♣K-J, he must surely have ♣A-Q-x-x-x-x which means that you have six clubs tricks, the ◇A and a spade trick – that's eight tricks even giving your partner just 6 points. Your partner is odds-on to provide a ninth trick and thus you should bid what you think you can make: 3NT.

The full deal is:

Dealer West. Game All.

```
              ♠ 8 2
              ♡ A 5 2
              ◇ 10 7
              ♣ A Q 10 9 8 4
♠ A K 10 9 7                    ♠ 6 5 4
♡ Q              N             ♡ K J 4 3
◇ K J 6 3     W     E          ◇ Q 9 8 5 2
♣ 7 3 2            S           ♣ 5
              ♠ Q J 3
              ♡ 10 9 8 7 6
              ◇ A 4
              ♣ K J 6
```

Your partner has a good overcall, but he would not be any weaker than this and should certainly have the six-card suit. If the opponents try to establish their spades, the obvious line of attack, then you will get home : your nine tricks will be six clubs, two aces and a spade trick.

But what if they attack diamonds? Unfortunately you are then one off in 3NT, but all is not lost for, as so often on this sort of deal, you still earn a good score. East-West can make 3♠ in comfort, so -100 would be reasonable against their 140. Perhaps more important is the comparison between a club contract and a no-trump contract: you make exactly the same number of tricks as 3♣ goes one off too! Your running suit provides the same tricks in no-trumps as it does in clubs, but of course the value of the tricks is so much greater in no-trumps.

Admittedly any lead except a low spade, or a top spade and spade continuation, will beat the contract, but most of the time the defence will lead their suit – which is generally the right action, otherwise we could bid 3NT without a stop!

If you know that, between you, you have a strong running minor, then if you have a stop in the opponents' suit think seriously about bidding no-trumps.

One stop
in the opponents' suit can
be enough for no-trumps

D o not be frightened of bidding no-trumps with just one stop in the opponents' suit; if your side has plenty of strength or a good source of tricks (a strong and long suit), then quite often one stop will suffice.

Obviously one would prefer a strong stop but holdings such as ♠A-5-4 or ♡K-3 will often be enough. In spades, the ace provides quite a good stop because you are able to hold up in the suit if necessary and thus might be safe even if you do not have nine tricks straight away. In hearts, your king looks rather precarious but, if the no-trump contract is first bid by you, it will be protected from attack since the lead will come round to your king. Of course there is a danger involved: if the opponents manage to lead another suit and fire a heart through your holding, you may finish rather a lot down, but how likely is it? Opponents usually lead their bid suit – for good reason too – and even if they do choose another suit, how likely is it that your right-hand opponent will have an entry if he wasn't the bidder?

To obtain better scores at duplicate bridge, especially pairs, it is important to take risks on bidding no-trump games. Take a look at this example.

You are South holding:

```
♠ A 3
♡ K 6
♢ A 8 5 4
♣ Q 10 6 3 2
```

It is Game All and the auction starts:

West	North	East	South
3♠	Dbl	Pass	?

North's double is for take-out.

With West holding a seven-card suit, your ace may not seem much of a stop, but there are two things that may happen in 3NT: (i) you could hold up your ace and hopefully cut West off from his partner, or (ii) with your combined strength you might have nine tricks on top. Things could go wrong and you could go a long way off, but it is certainly a risk worth taking. After all, pre-empts are designed to make your life awkward and this one has simply achieved its goal!

If the full deal is as below:

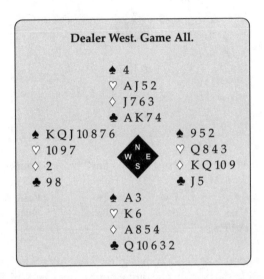

Dealer West. Game All.

	♠ 4	
	♡ A J 5 2	
	♢ J 7 6 3	
	♣ A K 7 4	
♠ K Q J 10 8 7 6		♠ 9 5 2
♡ 10 9 7		♡ Q 8 4 3
♢ 2		♢ K Q 10 9
♣ 9 8		♣ J 5
	♠ A 3	
	♡ K 6	
	♢ A 8 5 4	
	♣ Q 10 6 3 2	

On this occasion you cannot break communications in the spade suit, but you do have nine tricks on top: five clubs, the ♡A-K, the ♠A and the ♢A. Note that 5♣ is a reasonable contract, but you will probably go one off (5♣ can scrape home if declarer guesses who has the ♡Q and manages the complicated ending carefully). As so often, 3NT is worth the risk because the higher game is likely to fail.

Here is another example from a more competitive deal:

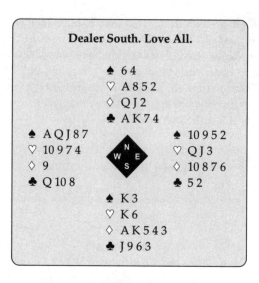

Dealer South. Love All.

```
            ♠ 6 4
            ♡ A 8 5 2
            ◊ Q J 2
            ♣ A K 7 4
♠ A Q J 8 7              ♠ 10 9 5 2
♡ 10 9 7 4              ♡ Q J 3
◊ 9                     ◊ 10 8 7 6
♣ Q 10 8               ♣ 5 2
            ♠ K 3
            ♡ K 6
            ◊ A K 5 4 3
            ♣ J 9 6 3
```

West	North	East	South
			1◊
1♠	Dbl	2♠	Pass
Pass	3♣	Pass	3NT
All Pass			

North has a good hand and knows game is on after South has opened the bidding. He starts with a negative double over 1♠, which shows his four-card heart suit, but when the auction comes back to him he is a little stuck. He bids the opponents' suit to show his strength and that he needs some help: North's main problem is that he has no stop in spades , so he wants to know if South can help him.

South does not have much of a spade stop, but with the lead coming up to him he can be sure that the ♠K will do its job; it might seem precarious, but it is worth risking 3NT. Your side certainly has the strength for game, and with no major-suit fit you should prefer 3NT to a minor-suit game as long as you have a stop of some sort.

There are ten easy tricks if West decides to lead a spade – the ♠K, five diamonds and two ace-kings – and nine top tricks if he leads another suit.

One stop is often enough, so you need to be bold when contemplating no-trump contracts.

Keep your two-level responses up to strength

Bidding systems are carefully structured for good reason: so that between the partnership you can accurately assess the level at which you should be playing as well as which denomination you should choose.

A two-level response to a one-level opening bid should show a hand worth at least 10 points. Some players like to raise this requirement further, some even play two-over-one as game-forcing, but in a relatively natural system the idea is that a two-level response shows more than the 1NT response, i.e. if you bid at the two level you have jumped over the 1NT barrier and so should have more points. The 1NT response shows 6-9 points, hence the two-level response shows 10 or more.

Why do you need this strength?

Well, if the opening bidder has a minimum 12 points and you have a misfit, then you should probably play in no-trumps, but if you bid to the two level with, say, 8 points, you cannot stop until 2NT, which will be much too high: just 20 points are unlikely to be enough to make eight tricks.

Have a look at this hand:

```
♠ 3
♡ 7 6
♢ A 8 5 4
♣ Q J 10 6 3 2
```

You are South and nobody is vulnerable:

West	North	East	South
	1♡	Pass	?

With just 7 points you must not toy with contemplating a response at the two level, but at the same time you must make a response. Use the "rubbish bin" response of 1NT; yes, ideally you would like to have a balanced hand, but it is more important to keep the bidding low.

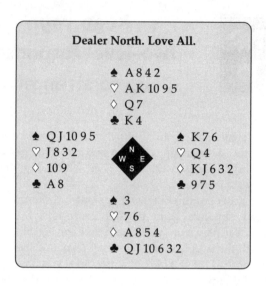

Dealer North. Love All.

```
              ♠ A 8 4 2
              ♡ A K 10 9 5
              ◇ Q 7
              ♣ K 4
♠ Q J 10 9 5              ♠ K 7 6
♡ J 8 3 2                 ♡ Q 4
◇ 10 9        N          ◇ K J 6 3 2
♣ A 8      W   E         ♣ 9 7 5
                S
              ♠ 3
              ♡ 7 6
              ◇ A 8 5 4
              ♣ Q J 10 6 3 2
```

Auction 1			
West	**North**	**East**	**South**
	1♡	Pass	1NT
Pass	2NT	Pass	3♣
All Pass			

Auction 2			
West	**North**	**East**	**South**
	1♡	Pass	2♣
Pass	2♠	Pass	3♣
Pass	3◇	Pass	3NT
All Pass			

Notice how quickly things get out of hand in Auction 2 when you give a two-over-one response: North "knows" that game is on (he has 16 points and South has shown 10+) so he continues over 2♣ first by showing his second suit, then by using the fourth suit to try and find a no-trump contract. North's bidding is faultless and if you give South the ♠K, 3NT is fine. Without the extra high card 3NT will go off, because the defence will make their spades.

Auction 1 is much more controlled. With a good 16 points, North tries for game by bidding 2NT. South should then bid 3♣ which neatly describes his hand: "I have at least six clubs but a weak hand, hence I could not respond 2♣." Now North should pass and 3♣ would gain the best score as there are nine easy tricks.

Use your normal methods in response to a 1NT overcall

It is important to have an accurate method when responding to your usual 1NT opening. Most players use Stayman and a lot of players also use Transfers. You should use these same methods when responding to a 1NT overcall, and for the same reasons: to give you flexibility, to help you find a 4-4 fit in a major, and to try to conceal the stronger hand. These methods work in exactly the same way as they do over a normal 1NT opening; indeed, you do best to ignore your opponent's opening bid altogether.

Here are two layouts which demonstrate the need for sticking to your normal methods:

Layout 1

♠ KQ43   ♠ AJ65
♡ AK6   ♡ 32
◇ A754   ◇ K986
♣ 63   ♣ Q82

West	North	East	South
			1♡
1NT	Pass	2♣	Pass
2♠	Pass	4♠	All Pass

West overcalls South's opening bid with 1NT, showing a balanced hand with 15-18 points and a good heart stop. East can be sure of game with his 10 points, but which game?

If his partner has four-card spade support, 4♠ is likely to be the best game, so he investigates by bidding 2♣, Stayman. West does indeed have four spades; he responds 2♠ and is raised to 4♠. The spade game should make easily while 3NT is in danger because of the club weakness.

Layout 2 shows how the flexibility of Jacoby Transfers can solve responder's problems:

Layout 2

♠ K 3		♠ A Q J 6 5
♡ A K 6	N	♡ 3 2
◊ Q J 5 4	W E	◊ 10 9 8
♣ K Q 6 3	S	♣ J 8 2

West	North	East	South
			1♡
1NT	Pass	2♡[1]	Pass
2♠[2]	Pass	2NT	Pass
3NT	All Pass		

[1] Transfer to spades
[2] West complies

Once again West overcalls 1♡ with 1NT, but this time East has a different quandary: he has 8 points so there is a chance of game, but which game? He would like to suggest spades as a contract and at the same time *invite* game. Transfers make East's life easy: he bids 2♡ to show his five-card spade suit and over West's forced 2♠ response he rebids 2NT. This all adds up to saying: "Partner, I have five spades and I think we have a chance for game."

West then assesses his own hand: with 18 points he can be sure that game is on, but with just a doubleton spade, no-trumps will be better than spades, hence he raises to 3NT. This contract will be easy, but in 4♠ you could fall foul of a diamond ruff, so the no-trump game is certainly safest.

As you can see, your conventions work perfectly well over a 1NT overcall and are certainly just as useful.

Don't overcall just because you have opening points

TIP 18

Too many players pick up a hand of 12-14 points with no five-card suit and feel that they have to bid. As the opening bidder you should certainly start proceedings, but as an overcaller you should be wary: most of these hands are surprisingly weak because they have no shortage or length, and will often have eight losers. If you play a 12-14 1NT opening, it is no surprise that it is called a *weak* no-trump.

Remember that an overcall should show at least *five* cards and therefore you would only be left with a choice of three calls: double, 1NT or pass. *Double* suggests shortage in the opponents' suit and a willingness to play in the three unbid suits – if you have a balanced hand you would be giving the wrong message; 1NT shows a strong hand, 15-18 points, so is not suitable either. Generally the best action on such hands after an opponents' opening bid is to *pass*.

Here is a typical hand; sitting South, vulnerable against non-vulnerable opponents, you are contemplating a bid, when East opens 1♡:

```
♠ A 8 4 3
♡ K 8 4
♦ Q J 6 4
♣ K 6
```

The bidding may proceed as in either of the following auctions:

Auction 1					Auction 2			
West	**North**	**East**	**South**		**West**	**North**	**East**	**South**
		1♡	Pass				1♡	Dbl
1♠	Pass	2♦	All Pass		1♠	2♣	All Pass	

Which South did best? Look at the full deal:

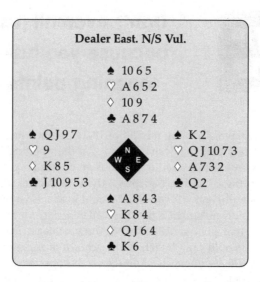

Dealer East. N/S Vul.

```
              ♠ 10 6 5
              ♡ A 6 5 2
              ◇ 10 9
              ♣ A 8 7 4
♠ Q J 9 7                    ♠ K 2
♡ 9              N           ♡ Q J 10 7 3
◇ K 8 5     W       E       ◇ A 7 3 2
♣ J 10 9 5 3     S           ♣ Q 2
              ♠ A 8 4 3
              ♡ K 8 4
              ◇ Q J 6 4
              ♣ K 6
```

As so often in misfitting part-score deals, whoever has to play the hand ends up going down; thus those players who are happy not to bid with the South hand will get a good score.

Whether East rebids 2◇ or 1NT (if it can show a weak hand) he should be comfortably defeated in whichever contract he finishes in. Meanwhile, if South wanders into the auction the only result is likely to be negative. In Auction 2, the take-out double gets the not-unexpected club reply (you are supposed to have support for that suit!) and South would do best to go to the bar rather than watch the result. A 1♠ overcall is just as bad because North will raise to 2♠, expecting a five-card suit.

I always advocate an aggressive bidding style; it is important to get into an auction if you can, but only for the right reasons. If you have a good five-card suit, you overcall; with shortage in the opponent's suit, you can double, and with a strong balanced hand you can overcall 1NT. However, when you have a weaker balanced hand you need to have patience: you will either find your partner making a bid "for you" later in the auction, borrowing a king for example (see Tip 5), or you will be able to use your hand in defence. Experience shows that 12-14 point balanced hands tend to be reasonable in defence with their all-round strength, but they tend to be pretty mediocre when it comes to declaring a suit contract.

Do not just bid for the sake of bidding; just because you are dealt opening strength does not mean you have to make a bid after the opponents have opened the auction.

Tips for Better Bridge

Overcalls can be quite weak, so be prudent when responding

Being able to enter the auction with a good five-card suit is important: it allows you to find the best lead; it allows you to find good fits and perhaps sacrifices, and it also allows you to compete each hand fully. A hand such as the one below has a perfectly reasonable overcall over a 1◇ opening bid:

> ♠ A K 8 4 3
> ♡ 4
> ◇ Q 6 4
> ♣ 9 8 6 4

A 1♠ overcall shows your five spades; it asks partner to lead a spade; and it also gets in the way of the opponents, making it more difficult for them to bid hearts. All in all, an excellent bid.

Note should be taken of the hand's all-round strength. Clearly it is a full trick less than an opening bid; it will play reasonably when you have a spade fit, but in any other contract it is likely to be worth just two tricks.

It is important for your partner to tread carefully; with support he can carry on bidding aggressively, but with no support he needs to be careful:

> ♠ 2
> ♡ K Q 9 5
> ◇ A 8 7 2
> ♣ A J 10 2

With this hand, after partner's 1♠ overcall too many players would get over-excited and finish in 3NT. When you hold a good hand, you should make a bid in the opponents' suit to show your strength, e.g.

West	North	East	South
			1◊
1♠	Pass	2◊	

2◊ means you have a strong hand and you want your partner to bid again. If he has a weak hand he should simply rebid his original suit at the lowest level; with a stronger hand he should rebid something else. So with the hands on the previous page (repeated below for convenience):

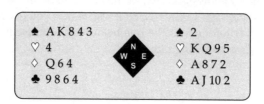

♠ AK843
♡ 4
◊ Q64
♣ 9864

♠ 2
♡ KQ95
◊ A872
♣ AJ102

The auction would continue:

West	North	East	South
			1◊
1♠	Pass	2◊	Pass
2♠	Pass	2NT	All Pass

2NT is not a great contract, but it is certainly a lot better than 3NT!
Change the West hand a little:

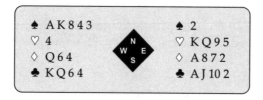

♠ AK843
♡ 4
◊ Q64
♣ KQ64

♠ 2
♡ KQ95
◊ A872
♣ AJ102

Now the overcaller has a hand with opening values, so in response to the 2◊ bid he would rebid 3♣ and the full auction would be:

West	North	East	South
			1◊
1♠	Pass	2◊	Pass
3♣	Pass	3NT	All Pass

Try not to punish your partner for making good aggressive overcalls.

Weak overcalls must be based on strong suits

You should always have good reasons for making an overcall and when you are weak there can only be one reason: you have a strong and long suit. If your partner can rely on the quality of your suit, that will help him judge in the play and in the auction.

Knowing that partner has a strong suit can help in a number of ways: (i) it makes your choice of lead easier (you need not be tempted by a suit of your own because partner will have a holding that is worthwhile leading to); (ii) it can help to select the final contract (with a high honour in partner's suit, you could count on a solid suit and try for no-trumps (see Tip 14); and (iii) it may even enable you to punish your opponents with a double.

How do you know whether your partner is weak? Well, if you have 7 or 8 points and the opponents bid on to game, then if your partner has overcalled he is only likely to have 7 or 8 points, in which case he should have a very good suit and you should rely on him to have it.

Take a look at the hand below and see if you can make use of your partner's overcall. You are South, holding:

♠ K 3
♡ A K 9
♢ 9 6 4 2
♣ 8 7 5 3

With East-West Vulnerable, you hear the auction proceed:

West	North	East	South
1♢	1♠	2♡	Pass
3♡	Pass	4♡	?

What on earth has your partner bid on? He does not appear to have many points , hence he should have an excellent suit. Playing duplicate pairs you have an excellent doubling hand: you trust your partner to have a good suit, and so you double and lead the ♠K. The full deal is:

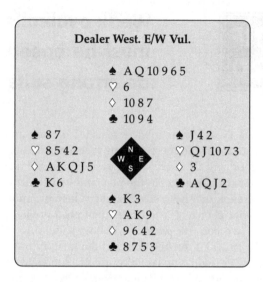

Dealer West. E/W Vul.

```
             ♠ A Q 10 9 6 5
             ♡ 6
             ◇ 10 8 7
             ♣ 10 9 4
♠ 8 7                          ♠ J 4 2
♡ 8 5 4 2         N            ♡ Q J 10 7 3
◇ A K Q J 5   W     E          ◇ 3
♣ K 6             S            ♣ A Q J 2
             ♠ K 3
             ♡ A K 9
             ◇ 9 6 4 2
             ♣ 8 7 5 3
```

On this layout you can take the first three tricks (West cannot overruff your ♡9) and you still have the ace-king of trumps! That's +500 for two down doubled and vulnerable.

Some tournament players will use jump bids to show weak hands like North's above, but playing a natural system you have to allow your one-level overcalls to have a wide range. North has good reason for overcalling: not only does he want the suit led, but he feels that if he can find a fit, then he may be able to find a sacrifice against 4♡ because of the favourable vulnerability. Change the South hand to the one below, for instance:

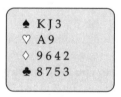

```
♠ K J 3
♡ A 9
◇ 9 6 4 2
♣ 8 7 5 3
```

Now 4♡ will make comfortably, but North-South would compete to 4♠. This contracts only makes seven tricks, but at the vulnerability that only costs -500 for three down doubled, instead of -620 for 4♡.

Aggressive overcalling can pay dividends in many different ways, but make sure, if you do overcall on a weak hand, that you have a good strong suit.

6NT requires 33 points not 4 aces and 4 kings

W hen you have a big fit, and therefore a lot of trumps, you can make extra tricks either by ruffing in both hands, or by ruffing long suits good. These trick-making techniques are not available in no-trump contracts and thus you have to rely on brute strength. High-card points are the key, and 33 points is generally the minimum you require for 6NT to be viable.

The number of aces and kings is not so important in no-trump contracts: four aces and four kings only make eight tricks. What is important is the all-round high-card point strength. What you will find is that your jacks and queens become very valuable, because when they are alongside kings and aces they will often have the same worth. ♠A-K-Q-J will make four tricks, the same as two ace-king combinations.

Here is your hand:

```
♠ K 8 5
♡ 10 3
♢ A J 6 5
♣ K 8 4 2
```

Your partner opens 2NT, showing 20-22 points and a balanced hand. What do you respond?

With a balanced hand with no five-card suit and no four-card major you should look no further than no-trumps for your denomination, but how high should you bid?

Your point total between the two hands is 31-33. If your partner has a maximum for his opening bid, you should have a good chance of making 6NT. The way to ask your partner this question is to bid 4NT. This is *not* Blackwood: it is a quantitative bid, asking partner to pass if he is minimum, or bid 6NT if he is maximum. The raise to 4NT works in a very similar fashion to a raise of 1NT to 2NT, inviting the opener to bid on if he has a maximum hand.

Consider the following examples:

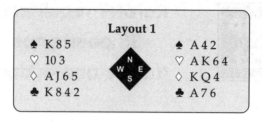

Layout 1

♠ K 8 5   ♠ A 4 2
♡ 10 3   ♡ A K 6 4
◇ A J 6 5   ◇ K Q 4
♣ K 8 4 2   ♣ A 7 6

West	East
	2NT
4NT	Pass

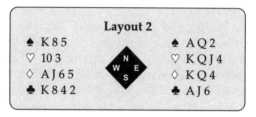

Layout 2

♠ K 8 5   ♠ A Q 2
♡ 10 3   ♡ K Q J 4
◇ A J 6 5   ◇ K Q 4
♣ K 8 4 2   ♣ A J 6

West	East
	2NT
4NT	6NT
Pass	

On *Layout 1* the opening bidder has a bare 20 points, and so passes 4NT – ten tricks are the limit when the clubs break 4-2. Notice that you actually hold all the aces and all the kings, but with not enough queens and jacks to back them up, you cannot get near a slam.

On *Layout 2* East has a maximum 22-count and therefore bids on to 6NT. This time you are missing an ace between you, but the queens and jacks more than make up for its absence – twelve tricks are straightforward.

An immediate raise of a no-trump bid to 4NT is usually played as quantitative, asking partner to assess his hand and bid on if he is maximum for his bidding thus far. The reason is precisely because the number of aces and kings is not so important, and thus when bidding 6NT Blackwood is usually not required.

Raise immediately, if weak with four-card support

When partner opens the bidding in a major, you should raise his suit immediately if you are weak with four-card support. This is important for two reasons:

1. You can give an accurate description of your hand to your partner (by making a limit bid).
2. By raising the level of the bidding quickly, you make it more difficult for your opponents to enter the auction.

"But surely with a five-card suit one should show it?" you might be asking.

The answer is no. Generally during an auction you only mention features that will be helpful; if you have already found a good fit in a major suit, why should you need to talk about another suit?

After all, the main reason for bidding suits is to find the best fit. Once you have found a good fit, you can stop showing your suits and instead show the strength of your hand.

Note that by a "weak" hand I mean a hand that cannot be sure that game is on – 11 or fewer points. With a hand of 12 or more points, you will often want to show your all-round strength and thus taking your time in the bidding has much more merit.

Here is a hand where you are faced with such a choice:

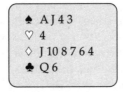

    ♠ A J 4 3
    ♡ 4
    ◊ J 10 8 7 6 4
    ♣ Q 6

You are South and your side is vulnerable. Your partner, North, is the dealer and opens 1♠. East passes. You do have a lovely long diamond suit, but I am not sure you should be letting your thoughts go towards it; concentrate on what really matters. What would you call?

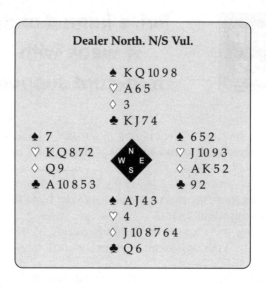

Dealer North. N/S Vul.

♠ K Q 10 9 8
♡ A 6 5
◇ 3
♣ K J 7 4

♠ 7
♡ K Q 8 7 2
◇ Q 9
♣ A 10 8 5 3

♠ 6 5 2
♡ J 10 9 3
◇ A K 5 2
♣ 9 2

♠ A J 4 3
♡ 4
◇ J 10 8 7 6 4
♣ Q 6

Auction 1			
West	North	East	South
	1♠	Pass	3♠
Pass	4♠	All Pass	

Auction 2			
West	North	East	South
	1♠	Pass	2◇
2♡	Pass	3♡	3♠
4♡	4♠	Pass	Pass
5♡	All Pass		

Compare these two auctions. Auction 1 is direct and accurate, and gets North-South the best score: +620 for 4♠ making. South has just 8 high-card points, but when you have a fit you can add points for distribution; here the singleton takes your hand to the intermediate range and you should therefore respond 3♠ rather than 2♠. The same goes for North: with his singleton, his hand is no longer a minimum and thus he has enough strength to bid game at the end of an excellent auction.

However, as so often on deals where both sides have a good fit, each side can make a surprising number of tricks; if you give East-West the chance to find their fit, then your auction will be less precise and may bring a nasty surprise at the end. In Auction 2, South's 2◇ bid is an error of judgment (also, he has not read Tip 16!) and West leaps at the chance to enter the auction. Now what does South's 3♠ bid mean? Three cards in spades? Is he competing or is he trying for game? Accuracy has been lost.

Not only has accuracy been lost, but at the vulnerability East-West can take advantage of your generosity and bid to 5♡. You will double this with high expectations, but even though you take it two down +300 is poor recompense for the +620 you should have been scoring.

In a competitive auction, show support immediately

TIP 23

Knowing that partner has support for your suit can transform your hand; quite often that is the reason why you make an overcall, just to find out whether your partner has support for you. If he does, you can get excited and bid high; if he doesn't, you can go back into hiding. To be able to bid thin games, or to find aggressive sacrifices, you need to have a partner who is willing to show support as much as he can. Remember that it is not so much the strength of your hand that matters, but cards in your partner's suit and a little distribution.

Here is your hand:

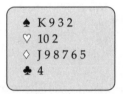

♠ K 9 3 2
♡ 10 2
◊ J 9 8 7 6 5
♣ 4

You are sitting South, with neither side vulnerable. The bidding starts:

West	North	East	South
1♡	1♠	3♡	?

Your first thought may well be: "But I only have four points!" However, you need to look beyond just your high-card point strength. With a fit, your hand gains strength from its distribution, and, perhaps even more importantly, if you are able to tell partner of your fit, then his hand will gain in strength too.

Showing support for partner should promise very little strength; what it should do is show your support and a little distribution.

The reason I keep using the expression "a little distribution" is because, with a flat hand, you do not want to push your partner into bidding on, because your hand will be worth very little – whilst with a hand like the one above, you will be able to bolster his trump suit as well as ruff clubs for him. Take a look at the full deal overleaf:

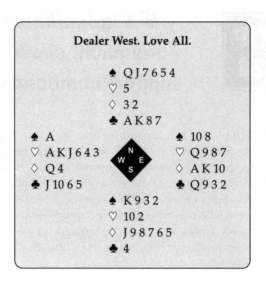

Dealer West. Love All.

♠ Q J 7 6 5 4
♡ 5
◊ 3 2
♣ A K 8 7

♠ A
♡ A K J 6 4 3
◊ Q 4
♣ J 10 6 5

♠ 10 8
♡ Q 9 8 7
◊ A K 10
♣ Q 9 3 2

♠ K 9 3 2
♡ 10 2
◊ J 9 8 7 6 5
♣ 4

West	North	East	South
1♡	1♠	3♡	3♠
4♡	4♠	Pass	Pass
5♡	All Pass		

Had you passed, then East-West would have finished in 4♡ making for 420 points. However, by bidding you allowed North to bid on to 4♠, which is a brilliant sacrifice bid: you go one off, but even if doubled that will only cost 100 points. But there is even better news in the auction because West, not unreasonably, bids on with 5♡, trying to secure his game bonus. This finishes the auction and North leads ♣A-K and a third club to defeat 5♡ by one trick and give your side a well-deserved +50 and an excellent score.

All because you bravely showed your support immediately with your 4-point hand!

Bid to the level of your fit quickly with weak hands

When you have a big fit, you will often make many more tricks than you expect. This is because as long as both hands have a little distribution, you will be able to use the excess trumps in each hand to ruff in both.

The expression "level of your fit" refers to the total number of cards between your two hands in your suit; if, for example, you both have a five-card suit, then your fit is ten cards and you should bid to make ten tricks – bid to the four level.

Once again the reason for bidding quickly is to stop the opponents having an accurate discussion and therefore stop them finding their optimum contract.

Here is an example:

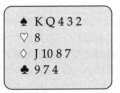

♠ K Q 4 3 2
♡ 8
◇ J 10 8 7
♣ 9 7 4

You are South, neither side is vulnerable and the auction starts:

West	North	East	South
1♡	1♠	2◇	?

What do you call?

Once again you are looking at a relatively weak hand, but you do have tremendous support for your partner's overcall. With good distribution too, you should follow my tip and bid to the level of your fit. Your partner's overcall has promised five cards and you also have five cards, which makes a total of ten, and so you should bid to contract for ten tricks – bid 4♠.

The full deal is:

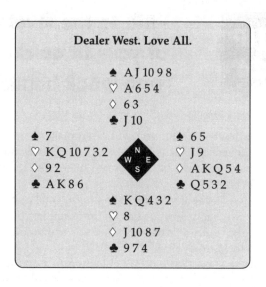

Dealer West. Love All.

```
                    ♠ A J 10 9 8
                    ♡ A 6 5 4
                    ◇ 6 3
                    ♣ J 10
    ♠ 7                              ♠ 6 5
    ♡ K Q 10 7 3 2     N            ♡ J 9
    ◇ 9 2            W   E          ◇ A K Q 5 4
    ♣ A K 8 6          S            ♣ Q 5 3 2
                    ♠ K Q 4 3 2
                    ♡ 8
                    ◇ J 10 8 7
                    ♣ 9 7 4
```

West	North	East	South
1♡	1♠	2◇	4♠
Pass	Pass	Dbl	All Pass

Look how difficult it makes it for East-West! What are they supposed to bid? They can probably make 5♡, but how are they to know that? They have no room for exchanging information! East can only really make a double, and hope they get you a few down. As there are four unavoidable losers in 4♠ (the rest can be ruffed), your bid has conceded just 100 points.

What a fantastic score that is when put against East-West's possible game score of 450!

Had you responded just 2♠, then East-West could have continued their conversation, and would then have had a better chance of bidding to 5♡ had you eventually bid to 4♠.

It may seem that you are taking a very great risk by bidding so high on so few points, but the power of a big fit can be trusted. Over time it has been proven that not only will a big fit supply a lot of tricks, but also that your opponents will have a fit themselves, so that if you do go down it is very likely that they would be able to make game themselves.

Bidding aggressively with big fits will bring you great rewards, but you must raise partner as early as you can!

Tips for Better Bridge

With strength and support, use the opponents' bid suit

TIP 25

The last few tips on support have shown you the importance of jumping quickly on weak hands, but that left the question of what to do when you have a strong hand with support. It is very important to distinguish between the two types, so when you hold a strong hand with support for your partner you should make a bid in the opponents' suit.

This type of bid takes getting used to, but the most important thing to understand is that you do not bid the opponents' suit because you want to play in it; you are actually bidding it for the opposite reason: to make sure that your partner makes another bid. It follows that, as you are forcing partner to bid again, (i) you must be strong to use a bid in the opponents' suit, and (ii) with just two suits bid, you also show good support for partner's suit.

As South, you hold:

> ♠ 7 4 3
> ♡ K Q 8 3
> ◇ A J 7 6
> ♣ K 4

Neither side is vulnerable and the auction starts:

West	North	East	South
	1♡	1♠	?

What do you call?

It certainly makes a change to be looking at a strong hand, but once again you have good support for your partner. It is tempting to bid 4♡, for you are pretty sure that it will make. However, partner is likely to put you with a weaker type of hand and will bid accordingly. To show a strong hand with support you should bid 2♠.

The full deal is over the page:

Dealer North Love All.

```
              ♠ —
              ♡ A J 6 5 4
              ◇ 8 5 3
              ♣ A Q J 10 7
♠ K Q 6 5 2                    ♠ A J 10 9 8
♡ 2              N             ♡ 10 9 7
◇ 10 9 2     W     E           ◇ K Q 4
♣ 9 8 6 5         S            ♣ 3 2
              ♠ 7 4 3
              ♡ K Q 8 3
              ◇ A J 7 6
              ♣ K 4
```

West	North	East	South
	1♡	1♠	2♠
4♠	5♣	Pass	5◇
Pass	6♡	All Pass	

What an excellent auction to a very good slam! The key is South's 2♠ call which suggests that he has a strong raise in hearts; now even over West's excellent barrage bid of 4♠ (in the style of Tip 24), North can try for a slam.

However, over a direct raise to 4♡, North will more than likely be thinking that 5♡ might be a sacrifice. He will have taken to heart Tips 22-24, and will remember the hand types on which you should be jumping to 4♡, many of them with just 4 or 5 points (just like West's here).

Using the opponents' suit to show your strength allows you to keep your partner in the picture, and enables your side to explore for slams when necessary. It also enables you to raise more freely on the weaker types of hand, because your partner will not expect too much strength since you did not bid the opponents' suit.

DECLARER-PLAY TIPS

When your contract depends on a finesse, think "endplay"

Rather than simply taking the 50-50 shot, try the effect of putting a defender on lead: they may have to lead the suit for you.

Endplay technique can be difficult; it consists of engineering the play so that you can neatly put a specific defender on lead at a crucial moment in order to force him to give you an extra trick. However, it can also be easy: by giving a defender the lead, you might find that they make a mistake or perhaps with a bit of luck they might be forced to give you a trick. Put simply: if you have a certain loser late in the play, try the effect of letting the defenders have that trick: quite often you will get a pleasant surprise.

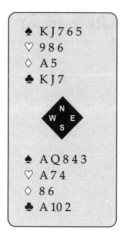

♠ K J 7 6 5
♡ 9 8 6
♢ A 5
♣ K J 7

♠ A Q 8 4 3
♡ A 7 4
♢ 8 6
♣ A 10 2

On the layout above, you finish in 4♠ and the ♡K is led. You are a little unlucky to find mirrored distribution, which means that there are only nine top tricks. However, you have a finesse for a tenth trick.

Without any special technique, what you can do is follow this tip: don't take the finesse until you have given the defence a chance to go wrong. Win the ♡A, draw trumps and cash the ◇A. Now give the defenders the lead. There is actually nothing the defenders can do: they win their three tricks (two hearts and one diamond), but then what? If they lead a club, they will catch the ♣Q for you, saving you the need

---

to finesse. If they return a red suit, then you are able to "ruff-and-discard", which means you can throw away your potential club loser while ruffing in the other hand – ten tricks made.

It did not matter who had the ♣Q; you made the contract without having to guess. There is of course some technique involved, but even without correct technique you can be rewarded for giving up the lead.

Endplay technique involves "eliminating" (i.e. exhausting) suits in preparation for a ruff-and-discard, and/or having suits with a "tenace" position (e.g. A-Q, K-J, Q-10, etc.). For example:

♠ KJ765
♡ 96
♢ A7
♣ KJ74

N
W E
S

♠ AQ843
♡ AK4
♢ 86
♣ A102

You are in 6♠ this time and West leads the ♢J. How do you play?

This hand fits with the theme; there are eleven "easy" tricks: five trumps, the ♡A-K, the ♢A, the ♣A-K and a heart ruff, therefore you require one more and a club finesse will supply it. But, as the tip says, you do not want to settle for a 50-50 shot, so your aim is to set the scene for an endplay: clubs are a finessable suit, but diamonds and hearts need to be eliminated first.

Win the ♢A, draw trumps, cash the ♡A-K and ruff a heart (the hearts are eliminated) and then play a diamond, giving the defenders the lead and at the same time eliminating diamonds.

It does not matter who wins the trick: the defence are well and truly endplayed. A red suit lead will allow you to ruff in the North hand and discard South's third club, while a club lead will allow you to pick up the queen. This time the endplay was neatly planned.

Whether you can craft an endplay, or are simply desperate, consider giving the defenders the lead before taking a last-ditch finesse.

Consider what a defender might be thinking about

One is supposed to play at an even tempo, but when you are faced with some difficult decisions, it is not so easy. You are welcome to spend as much time as you want thinking about your decisions, but be aware that your opponents can take advantage of your predicament.

In no-trumps, endplays (see Tip 26) are much rarer because there is no ruffing to be done, but sometimes you can find a neat endplay against a player when you can predict his cards. Often this will be because he has made a bid and so shown high-card-point strength, but the other time is when a defender struggles with his discards.

```
        ♠ 7 6 4
        ♡ J 6
        ◇ A K 8 7 6
        ♣ J 9 2

              N
          W       E
              S

        ♠ A Q
        ♡ A 2
        ◇ 5 4
        ♣ A K Q 6 5 4 3
```

On this layout, you are in 6NT against which West leads the ♡K. You win your ace and count your tricks: seven clubs, the ◇A-K and two more aces comes to eleven. You have a spade finesse for your twelfth trick. However, since the opponents have knocked out the ♡A, you cannot afford the tactic suggested in Tip 26 because if you give the opponents the lead they will cash their tricks! So it looks as though the contract will depend on the spade finesse. You start by cashing your long suit to see what happens. Nobody seems to have too much to think about, but when you cross to your two diamond winners, things change:

```
    ♠ 7
    ♡ J
    ◊ A K 8
    ♣ —

        N
     W     E
        S

    ♠ A Q
    ♡ 2
    ◊ 5 4
    ♣ —
```

West is starting to think laboriously; having discarded all his diamonds already he decides to throw the ♡7 on the ◊A, but when you play the ◊K, he slips into a trance, unable to decide what to do. Eventually he discards the ♡10.

Can you see what's happening? Each player has just three cards left – West has discarded on clubs and diamonds, and so only has major-suit cards left. What do you think they are?

Surely, since he is taking such a long time, he must have some reason to want to keep his spades. He must hold the ♠K.

This was the layout just before you led the ◊K (remember, West chose to discard the ♡10 on the ◊K):

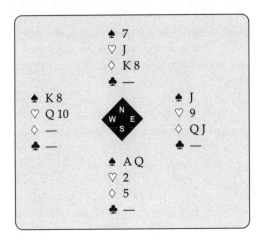

```
              ♠ 7
              ♡ J
              ◊ K 8
              ♣ —
    ♠ K 8                    ♠ J
    ♡ Q 10        N          ♡ 9
    ◊ —        W     E       ◊ Q J
    ♣ —           S          ♣ —
              ♠ A Q
              ♡ 2
              ◊ 5
              ♣ —
```

"Knowing" that West has the ♠K, you spurn the spade finesse and instead put West on lead by playing the ♡J. West is forced to lead away from his ♠K, and you make the last two tricks and your contract.

Here is the full deal:

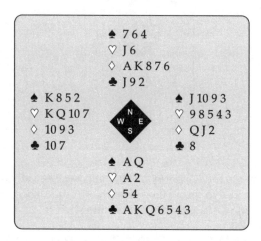

```
                    ♠ 7 6 4
                    ♡ J 6
                    ◇ A K 8 7 6
                    ♣ J 9 2
     ♠ K 8 5 2                      ♠ J 10 9 3
     ♡ K Q 10 7          N          ♡ 9 8 5 4 3
     ◇ 10 9 3        W       E      ◇ Q J 2
     ♣ 10 7              S          ♣ 8
                    ♠ A Q
                    ♡ A 2
                    ◇ 5 4
                    ♣ A K Q 6 5 4 3
```

This deal demonstrates two things: never rely solely on a finesse until all hope has gone and, more importantly, make your decisions early as a defender. West knew that declarer would play seven clubs and the ◇A-K, so he should have been ready for the discards and no matter how difficult they may have been, had he discarded smoothly (perhaps even baring his ♠K), you would have been unlikely to think that he had the ♠K and therefore would have taken the spade finesse and gone one off.

You are allowed to take advantage of your opponents' thinking and discomfort, so when you witness it, try to work out why they are taking their time: quite often this will show you the right line to take to fulfil your contract.

Always take
your time
at trick one

Make a plan: look at each suit in turn and assess how you will tackle it either on your lead or the opponents'. By doing this you will be ready for most eventualities and can often predict the problems before they surface.

When dummy is tabled, there is almost always a huge amount to take in. Both declarer and the defenders should take their time. The rules of bridge allow thinking time for all players to consider the dummy and make a plan (see page 112); after trick one, though, the play should be at a more even pace. Why should you take this extra time?

Because bridge is a very complex game. If you can plan ahead and predict problems, then you can play the right cards at the right time. If you do not see the problem until it happens, then it might be too late.

Let me give you an example of the kind of suit that can be easily overlooked in your plan:

♣ A K Q 8 5

♣ 10 9 2

With no outside entries to the North hand in a 3NT contract and needing all five tricks from the suit, you might think there is nothing to think about. Hoping that the suit breaks well, you lead up to the ♣A and follow with ♣K, but East discards. All is not lost, you reckon, for you can finesse West for the ♣J; so you cross to your hand and lead the ♣10, but West does not cover your card – and you cannot get to North's hand.

If you plan for a bad break "just in case", you can prepare for it by playing the ♣10-9 underneath the ♣A-K; now when you cross back to the South hand, you are able to lead the ♣2 and whatever West plays, you will be in dummy to enjoy all five clubs.

Now consider the following problem:

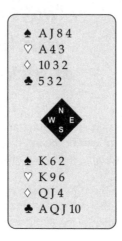

♠ A J 8 4
♡ A 4 3
◇ 10 3 2
♣ 5 3 2

♠ K 6 2
♡ K 9 6
◇ Q J 4
♣ A Q J 10

West	North	East	South
			1♣
1◇	1♠	Pass	1NT
Pass	3NT	All Pass	

You are South; playing a weak no-trump system you end up as declarer in 3NT. West leads the ◇7. How do you play?

Work your way through your plan:

1. Top tricks
2. Methods of establishment
3. Stops in the opponents' suit
4. Entries from hand to hand

Another thing to do is to look at each suit in isolation and see if there might be any oddities.

If you go through the plan each time, however tedious it might seem, then you should come up with the correct answer more often than not.

You have five top tricks here and are assured of a trick in diamonds, but the diamond lead means you will be out of stops. You need three more tricks; you can make a couple in spades, but that is not enough; clubs are the only suit in which you can establish three more tricks. This is risky because if West has the king he will be able to cash all his diamonds, but you have no choice and therefore you have to hope that East has the king.

But you are not finished yet – yes, you have decided that you are going to play on the club suit, but play it through in your head and count your entries. Cross to the ♡A and play a club to the ten; cross to the ♠A and play a club to the jack; if East has four clubs to the king, then you need another entry. So before playing to the first trick you have worked out that you could do with another entry if possible. You might be able to take a spade finesse to create the extra entry, but that is yet another risk. Is there a safe entry to dummy?

If West has not got the ♣K (that is what you hope) what does he have for his bid?

Most likely he has ace-king to five diamonds and is underleading the suit to keep communications between the defenders (after trick one, if either defender gets the lead, they will still have a diamond to lead).

That is a lot of thinking to have to do before you play a card but, having made your extended plan, you realise that the ◇10 might be your extra entry. The full deal is:

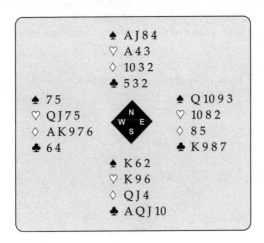

```
              ♠ A J 8 4
              ♡ A 4 3
              ◇ 10 3 2
              ♣ 5 3 2
♠ 7 5                        ♠ Q 10 9 3
♡ Q J 7 5      N             ♡ 10 8 2
◇ A K 9 7 6  W   E           ◇ 8 5
♣ 6 4          S             ♣ K 9 8 7
              ♠ K 6 2
              ♡ K 9 6
              ◇ Q J 4
              ♣ A Q J 10
```

You leap up with ◇10 at trick one and take a club finesse, then lead a heart to the ace and take another club finesse, finally you lead a spade to the ace and take a third club finesse; that makes four club tricks, one diamond and two ace-kings: nine tricks.

Plays such as these at trick one are not easy to spot, but the only chance you have of spotting them is if you take your time and you work your way through your plan.

Establish extra tricks before cashing your winners

A major part of the plan you make before the end of trick one should be adding your Top Tricks to those which you can establish in order to reach your target; the plan will then involve establishing the tricks and then eventually playing all the winners.

There are two good reasons for establishing before cashing out:

1. When you play your winners you will often establish cards for your opponents; e.g. you can cash an ace-king in a suit, but then the opponents' queen-jack will make.
2. Sometimes if you cash a long suit, you may struggle to find discards.

Here is a deal which illustrates point 2 above:

♠ A
♡ K 7 3
♦ A Q J 10 8 6 3
♣ K 3

♠ Q J 2
♡ J 10 5
♦ K 9 2
♣ J 8 4 2

West	North	East	South
	1◇	1♠	1NT
2♠	3NT	All Pass	

Your partner has taken a gamble on his diamond suit, and with you holding the king it should pay off. How do you play after the ♠8 lead?

You have eight top tricks, so you need just one more. One plan is to win the ♠A and run all your diamonds, but then you have to find four discards; you cannot afford a spade discard and you cannot really afford a heart discard, nor can you really afford more than one club discard – to sum it up, you cannot afford to cash your diamond suit. Another reason is, of course, that you need entries to South's hand and you have two available in the diamond suit.

Follow the tip: establish your ninth trick first. Win the ♠A, cross to the ◇9 and play the ♠Q. East wins his king while you safely discard a heart from dummy; he will probably play another spade, and you have done your work: with two spade tricks in the bag, you can cash your diamond suit for nine tricks. The full deal is:

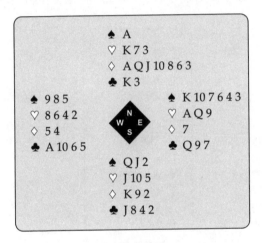

```
              ♠ A
              ♡ K 7 3
              ◇ A Q J 10 8 6 3
              ♣ K 3
  ♠ 9 8 5                      ♠ K 10 7 6 4 3
  ♡ 8 6 4 2         N          ♡ A Q 9
  ◇ 5 4         W     E        ◇ 7
  ♣ A 10 6 5        S          ♣ Q 9 7
              ♠ Q J 2
              ♡ J 10 5
              ◇ K 9 2
              ♣ J 8 4 2
```

Cashing a long suit can make life very difficult for your opponents, but before you cash out, make sure it won't make life even more difficult for you!

Making a plan at the start of play should always involve two essential calculations: how many top tricks do you have and how many tricks can you establish? Your aim is to make that total equal to or above your contract. To reach this total, you have to do the work to establish your tricks first, before playing winners.

Use your opponents' bidding to your advantage

There are so many things to think about when making a plan of play; one especially important factor is the opponents' bidding. They might be a nuisance during the auction, but opponents' bids can be very handy during the play. In fact, the lack of a bid can also be helpful.

A player who has opened will usually have 12 or more points; and a player who has passed as opener will have fewer than 12 points.

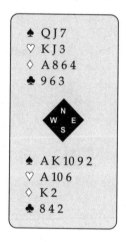

♠ Q J 7
♡ K J 3
◇ A 8 6 4
♣ 9 6 3

♠ A K 10 9 2
♡ A 10 6
◇ K 2
♣ 8 4 2

West	North	East	South
Pass	Pass	Pass	1♠
Pass	2◇	Pass	2♠
Pass	3♠	Pass	4♠
All Pass			

You are South, the declarer in 4♠. West leads the ♣A-K-Q, East following with the five, seven and ten; West then plays a trump.

The important factor on this deal is that West passed as dealer. He has shown up with a fantastic club suit: ♣A-K-Q-J, so surely if he had the ♡Q as well he would have opened the bidding. Having sussed this out, you place the ♡Q with East and play the hearts accordingly.

The full deal is:

```
            ♠ Q J 7
            ♡ K J 3
            ◇ A 8 6 4
            ♣ 9 6 3
♠ 8 5                          ♠ 6 4 3
♡ 7 5 4 2        N             ♡ Q 9 8
◇ 10 7 3      W     E          ◇ Q J 9 5
♣ A K Q J        S             ♣ 10 7 5
            ♠ A K 10 9 2
            ♡ A 10 6
            ◇ K 2
            ♣ 8 4 2
```

Here is another example:

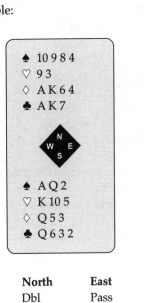

```
            ♠ 10 9 8 4
            ♡ 9 3
            ◇ A K 6 4
            ♣ A K 7

                  N
               W     E
                  S

            ♠ A Q 2
            ♡ K 10 5
            ◇ Q 5 3
            ♣ Q 6 3 2
```

West	North	East	South
1♡	Dbl	Pass	3NT
All Pass			

West starts with the ♡7, on which East plays the queen. You have 27 points between your two hands and East has turned up with the ♡Q, yet West opened the bidding. Clearly West must have all the outstanding points and thus the key to this hand is that there is no point taking a spade finesse because it is bound to lose.

Thus you should test the two minor suits hoping for a good break, but if you have no luck you will need a last resort. You win the first round of hearts and play diamonds followed by clubs (no luck, except that it is West that shows out in each suit, throwing a small spade each time). However, you do have that "last resort": knowing that West has only spades and hearts left, you can give him the lead – you exit with a heart to the nine. West does indeed have to win the trick and can cash four hearts in total, but at that point his fun ends since he has to return a spade into your ace-queen.

The full deal is:

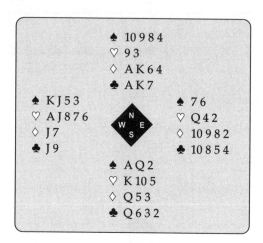

On this last layout, because you could be sure that West held the ♠K, you avoided the forlorn spade finesse and instead were able to endplay West, forcing him to lead a spade away from his "known" king.

West's opening bid was rather weak on the above deal, but it gave you all the help you needed! The auction certainly can be a very valuable aid to declarer play.

Avoid the "baddie" gaining the lead

Quite often during play you can choose the defender to whom you give the lead at any given time. When you make your original plan, you should consider which defender you would be happy to put on lead and which one would be dangerous. I like to label the defenders "goodie" and "baddie"! How do you know which is which?

Consider this holding:

Very precarious, but if you can avoid a lead through the king you will be much more secure. Thus North is the goodie, for if he obtains the lead, he cannot attack the suit without giving you a trick with your king. It follows that South is the baddie, because if he gains the lead he can lead a club straight through your king.

How about this one:

South leads the ◇K against your no-trump contract: who's the goodie and who's the baddie?

Although South is likely to hold the length in diamonds, you would prefer him to be on lead because after you win his king with your ace, he will not be able to continue the suit without giving a trick to your jack. However, a lead from North through your jack could be devastating.

Another common situation is when the defence have established a suit in a no-trump contract; the baddie is the player holding the remainder of the suit – if you can keep him off lead you might be able to avoid losing those tricks.

Take a look at the deal overleaf:

♠ 8 6 4
♡ 9 3
◇ 6 4
♣ A K Q J 5 4

♠ A Q J 10 9 5
♡ A 6 5
◇ K 8
♣ 10 3

West	North	East	South
			1♠
Pass	2♣	Pass	3♠
Pass	4♠	All Pass	

West leads the ♡Q against 4♠. Plan the play.

Once trumps are drawn there are plenty of winners (in clubs and spades), but what about the losers? In the worst case you could lose a spade, a heart and two diamonds. Consider which defender might be the baddie and which the goodie.

Diamonds are your weak suit: you cannot afford a lead through your king, so East is the baddie and West the goodie. What this means is that you should try to plan giving any tricks that you have to lose to West. In spades you are fortunate, because if East has the king you will have a successful finesse and if West has it you will not mind him winning it because he is the goodie, but what about the heart suit?

How can you make sure East does not win the defence's certain heart trick?

Duck the first trick, letting West win his ♡Q – it is as simple as that! Of course, if East plays the king you would have to win the trick, but then he wouldn't be able to gain the lead in hearts any more, as can be seen from the full deal:

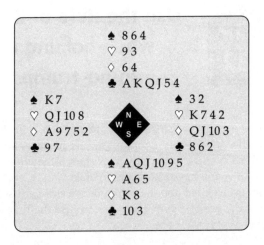

```
                    ♠ 8 6 4
                    ♡ 9 3
                    ◊ 6 4
                    ♣ A K Q J 5 4
   ♠ K 7                          ♠ 3 2
   ♡ Q J 10 8        N            ♡ K 7 4 2
   ◊ A 9 7 5 2     W   E          ◊ Q J 10 3
   ♣ 9 7             S            ♣ 8 6 2
                    ♠ A Q J 10 9 5
                    ♡ A 6 5
                    ◊ K 8
                    ♣ 10 3
```

You can win the second heart, ruff a third heart and take a spade finesse, and if West does not cash his ◊A now you will make an easy overtrick; after trumps are drawn all the clubs will win.

If you make the mistake of winning the first heart, then when West wins his ♠K he can play a heart over to East's king and East can then lead the ◊Q, killing your king and defeating 4♠ by one trick.

Considering which defender is the goodie and which is the baddie is a good habit to acquire; it will help you develop various declarer-play techniques, especially hold-up plays and avoidance plays. Hold-up plays (see Tip 32 for an example) are designed to break communications between the defenders (exhausting one player of a suit), so that there is only one baddie. These can often be followed up by avoidance plays, one of which was shown in our example above: plays which deliberately aim to avoid one player (the baddie) getting the lead.

Use the Rule of Seven when holding up in no-trumps

TIP 32

When you are short of stops in a particular suit, you should try to break the opponents' communications in order to stop them running their suit. This is especially important if they have a five-card suit, for then they will have four tricks to make, unless you are careful.

When you are worried about an opponent's five-card suit in which you have just the ace as a stop, then you can use the Rule of Seven to tell you when to play your ace.

THE RULE OF SEVEN

Add the number of cards in the suit in your hand and dummy's, and take away the total from seven – the answer tells you for how many rounds you should hold up.

So with this spade suit:

♠ 5 2

♠ A 6 4

If your left-hand opponent led the ♠K, the Rule of Seven would work in this way:

You have five cards between your two holdings, therefore you should hold up for (7-5) = two rounds.
Hence you duck the ♠K and then duck the ♠Q, winning the third round.

The rule can also work if you have the king and the defence take the ace on the first round:

♡ 9 8 7

♡ K 5 2

West leads the ♡4 to East's ace and he returns the ♡10.

Using the rule, you should hold up for one round (7-6). The first round has gone, so you should win trick two with your king.

Let us see how the rule works in action:

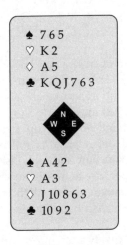

♠ 7 6 5
♡ K 2
◇ A 5
♣ K Q J 7 6 3

♠ A 4 2
♡ A 3
◇ J 10 8 6 3
♣ 10 9 2

West	North	East	South
	1♣	Pass	1◇
1♠	2♣	Pass	2NT
Pass	3NT	All Pass	

West leads the ♠K.

You have stretched a little and you are going to need a little luck to prevent West making his spade suit: if West has the ♣A there will be nothing you can do. However, if East has the ♣A, then you can prevail by breaking communications in the spade suit, so that when East wins the ♣A he will not be able to play a spade back.

Use the Rule of Seven: you have six cards, therefore you should hold up for just one round.

The full deal is over the page:

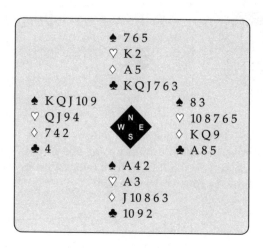

You win the second round of spades and knock out the ♣A – the rule works! East wins his ace, but cannot return a spade and you can therefore collect all your club tricks to make 3NT.

Why not hold up twice just in case?

A lazy declarer might indeed hold up twice, but he would be defeated by a more awake defender. After collecting two spades, West should give up on his spade suit and look elsewhere. He will guess that South has the ♡A otherwise he would surely not have held up so long; so he will try a diamond switch. With two spade tricks in the bank, the defence now establish two diamond tricks to go with their ♣A.

The Rule of Seven is relatively straightforward; trust it and contracts like this will become easy!

A low lead usually promises length and an honour

The defenders use leading methods to help the leader's partner assess how long and strong the suit led might be; you can use their methods to your advantage. The most common method is "fourth highest" – short for "fourth-highest card from an honour". Therefore when you see a small card led, you should bear in mind that the leader is likely to hold an honour. Quite often you will be able to take advantage of this later in the play.

Let's look at some suit combinations:

West leads the ♠5 and you should play low from dummy. You capture East's jack with your queen. You can now be pretty sure that West's king is stuck between your ace and ten; so later in the hand you should be able to take a successful finesse:

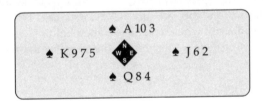

East can save the day for the defence (as you will see in Tip 52) by not playing his jack on the first trick, but what is most important is to take full advantage of the defence's mistakes.

In this suit you can take the logic a step further. West leads the ♡5 to the six, ten and queen.

If West has led fourth highest, then he must have started with J-9-7-5 because you can see all the other cards except the ♡4 – he might hold this card too if his suit is longer. What difference does this make?

Well, you can actually make all four heart tricks: you lead towards your A-K-8 and if West plays low you can confidently insert the eight; winning the trick. If West pops up with his nine, then you win the ace and cross back to hand to lead another heart; eventually West will give in and you make all four tricks in the suit, the layout being:

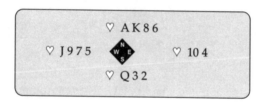

Making use of the opponents' leads is very important. The defenders gain a great deal by having accurate signals and lead conventions, but they can also give a great deal away. It is your job to take advantage of all the information you are given. As you can see, when your opponents lead a suit where you have a good holding, you must try to make the most of their misfortune by finessing for the missing cards.

When declaring 1NT try to be patient

A 1NT contract is notoriously difficult to play, but it is also very difficult to defend. The difficulties centre on the need for patience: with the points very often evenly divided, the honours will be spread, which makes for "frozen suits", i.e suits that neither side can profit from leading and therefore suits that both sides should avoid leading if possible. The result is that the side with greater patience wins!

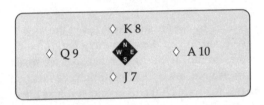

With eight diamonds left, see what happens when each player leads:

1. **West:** if he leads the queen, the king covers promoting the jack – one trick to North-South; if he leads small, dummy plays small and either the jack or king will make a trick – one trick to North-South.
2. **North:** the ◊K lead gets crushed and the jack can be crushed later – zero tricks to North-South; if North leads small, the ten is played and South's jack loses to the queen – zero tricks to North-South.
3. **East:** the ◊A lead allows the king to make, and a small lead runs round to the king – one trick to North-South.
4. **South:** the ◊J gets covered along with the king – zero tricks to North-South. The ◊7 lead is covered by the ◊9 and then the king gets killed by the ace – zero tricks to North-South.

Thus, if North-South lead the suit they will not make a trick, but if East-West lead the suit, North-South will make one trick.

So it is important to avoid leading suits where your side hold just two honours – one on each side of the table. This is where patience comes into it; if you wait long enough, the defenders will play the suit for you; or you might even be able to force them to lead it.

♠ J 3 2
♡ 8 6 4
◇ K Q 9 5
♣ Q 8 3

♠ K 8 4
♡ A K 2
◇ J 10 8 6
♣ A 10 2

The contract is 1NT by South and West leads the ♡Q. You appear to
have six relatively easy tricks: three top tricks and three diamond tricks.
What about your seventh? Both clubs and spades are frozen suits; if you
lead them yourself your lower honours might be crushed. So the first
part of the plan is to establish the diamond suit and the second part is
to put your opponents on lead. Now look at the full deal:

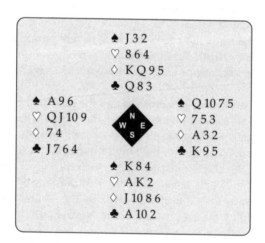

♠ J 3 2
♡ 8 6 4
◇ K Q 9 5
♣ Q 8 3

♠ A 9 6
♡ Q J 10 9
◇ 7 4
♣ J 7 6 4

♠ Q 10 7 5
♡ 7 5 3
◇ A 3 2
♣ K 9 5

♠ K 8 4
♡ A K 2
◇ J 10 8 6
♣ A 10 2

Win the ♡A, knock out the ◇A, win the heart return, cash your diamonds
and then play your last heart. West will win his two heart tricks but then
he has to play a club or a spade. A spade lead will allow your king to
make a trick, and a club lead will squash East's king under your ace and
allow an extra trick for the ♣Q. Either way you get your seventh trick.

Tips for Better Bridge

Duck an early round when you are short of entries

L ong suits are very useful in no-trump contracts – they can generate a lot of extra tricks – but to profit from those extra tricks you must be able to reach the hand that contains them.

Let me show you a few suits in isolation before looking at a full deal:

You have no entries to the South hand, so if you play the suit from the top ($\Diamond$A, $\Diamond$K, then a third round), you will lose the third trick and although you have established the last two diamonds you will have no way of reaching them.

Bearing this in mind, a good tactic is to duck an early round to keep communication between the two hands. Therefore you would let your opponents win the first diamond trick, but then you would play the $\Diamond$A and the $\Diamond$K on the second and third rounds, and when all the remaining diamonds fall you are still in the South hand in order to play off your two winning diamonds.

This technique also works with a slightly shorter suit, as illustrated on the next page:

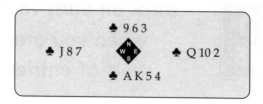

♣ 9 6 3

♣ J 8 7   ♣ Q 10 2

♣ A K 5 4

This club suit is very similar to the diamond suit on the previous page, but with no entries outside the club suit to the South hand you can still generate an extra trick with a well-timed duck. This time you will have to rely on a lucky break in the suit, but that is your only chance for an extra trick. Once again, if you cash your ace-king first and then play a third round, you will have no way of reaching your established ♣5; if instead you play small from both hands first, then you can win the second and third rounds with the ace and king, and remain in the South hand to score your last club.

Ducking in a suit to preserve communications is a good habit to acquire. It requires planning, most of which should take place at trick one – if you play too quickly it can be too late. Try this deal:

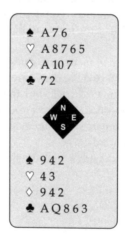

♠ A 7 6
♡ A 8 7 6 5
◇ A 10 7
♣ 7 2

♠ 9 4 2
♡ 4 3
◇ 9 4 2
♣ A Q 8 6 3

You are declarer in 1NT and you receive the ♠K lead.

Four top tricks and the rest is looking ugly! There is a little chance for extra tricks in your two long suits, but your hearts are very weak, so it will have to be the clubs. However, there is no entry to your club suit other than in the suit itself. You are going to need some luck, but it is your best chance; you have to hope that clubs break 3-3 and that East has the ♣K. But that's not all: it is no good taking the club finesse, because even if it works you will have no entries to the suit. The answer, as I am sure you have guessed, is to play small from both hands on the first round of clubs, then when you eventually get the lead again, you will take the finesse, leaving you in the right hand to enjoy the whole suit.

The full deal is:

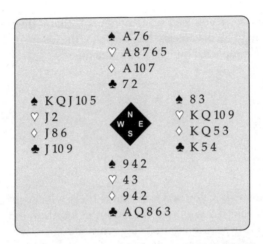

Using the Rule of Seven (Tip 32) you duck one round of spades and win the second, and you play exactly as you have planned above: a small club from both hands. West wins his ♣9 and can cash all his spades, but you can win his switch with an ace in dummy and play a second club inserting your queen; when this holds the trick, you can cash the ace and breathe a sigh of relief as the honours come tumbling down. You take two more club tricks to scrape home in your contract.

This deal shows another important element of 1NT play: you need not be so worried about the defence establishing one suit, but should try to avoid it happening in two suits. Basically you can afford to lose six tricks, so there is no great need to thwart the establishment of the spade suit and thus you are not nervous about giving up the lead in clubs – four spade tricks are a manageable loss.

Entry-preservation plays are surprisingly common and they should be easy to spot, although perhaps not so easy to perform! Whenever you see a long suit in a weak hand your focus should be drawn to how you are going to establish the suit and reach it. Of course, it is not so problematical if the long suit is in the strong hand because there will be plenty of entries to go with it.

Lead up to your two-honour holding

The reason why you lead up to honours is that if the first defender plays a high card, you can then duck, for the loss of no high card of your own. A simple example is a suit like this:

If the suit breaks 3-3, you will make three tricks whatever happens, but if the suit breaks 4-2 you may well lose the fourth round, unless you can avoid one of your honours being crushed.

The best way to play the suit is to lead towards the king first and, if that holds, cross back to the South hand to lead towards the queen again. It wins when the suit divides as below:

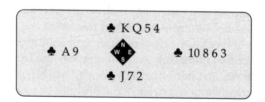

The first trick is won by the king and then when you lead from the South hand a second time, West has to play his ace and you can play small. By making the defenders "waste" their ace, each of your three honours makes a trick.

Playing this way may also gain if the defenders make a mistake with the layout of the suit as shown on the next page:

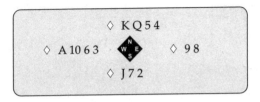

The defenders should make two tricks if you play on this suit, but you can put West under pressure, by leading towards your two honours. It is easy for a defender to duck once, but many defenders find it difficult to duck twice. If you start with the ◇2 to the ◇K and then cross over to lead the ◇7, you will be amazed by the number of defenders who will fall at this second hurdle and play their ace.

This kind of play is correct with most combinations of three honours when they are split between declarer and dummy's hands:

It might seem obvious to take a finesse by leading the ♡Q but that wastes your queen: it will be killed by the king and even though you can then kill that with your ace, you will be left with two losers when the suit breaks 4-2.

Remember that your aim is to protect your honours, so lead up to your two-honour holding by playing the ♡2 to the queen, then crossing to the ace and leading the ♡7. This allows you to make three tricks whenever West has the king.

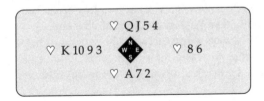

West's king cannot kill your queen or jack, as long as you lead up to them.

Here is a similar combination of honours:

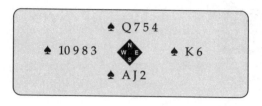

Once again, the correct play is to lead small to the two-honour combination. Therefore you lead the ♠4 to the jack. When this wins the trick, you can play the ♠A which brings down the king, allowing you to make three tricks. If you lead the queen instead, it will be killed by the king, leaving just two winners.

Here is one final layout:

"Surely you do not want me to lead away from my king towards the jack-ten?" I hear you say.

It depends on your aims. If you are trying to establish the suit, then yes, you should do exactly that – it gives the best chance of making two tricks in the suit. However, if you are looking for one quick trick, then you might play the suit in a different way. Notice once again how futile a finesse is when your intermediates are so weak. The queen is bound to kill either the ten or jack, and with the king falling to the ace there is only one trick for you if you broach the suit from the North hand. Lead away from your king and you have your best chance: the first lead to the jack is taken by East's queen, but once again you lead away from your king and now West's ace takes two low cards and your honours are preserved to take the last two tricks in the suit.

Your aim is always to protect your honours and hope that you can force the defence to waste their high cards. One of the best ways to attempt this is by leading towards two-honour holdings.

Do not always assume a suit will break well

Bridge would be a much easier game if we could rely on a good break in all the suits. However, it is important to try to cope with bad breaks, and quite often it is necessary to plan early. Hence, when you find yourself in a relatively straightforward contract, you should consider whether you would be able to cope with a bad break and plan accordingly.

For example:

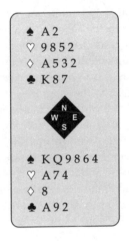

♠ A 2
♡ 9 8 5 2
◇ A 5 3 2
♣ K 8 7

♠ K Q 9 8 6 4
♡ A 7 4
◇ 8
♣ A 9 2

You are South in 4♠ and West leads the ♡K. How would you play?

Things look easy: six trumps, the ♡A, the ◇A and the ♣A-K – ten tricks. But what happens if trumps break 4-1?

Down to nine tricks, you will need to make one more. You have a small chance in hearts (if the suit breaks 3-3), but is there anything else?

You can actually still make six trump tricks even if they break 4-1: the ace, king and queen, and three diamond ruffs. To get three diamond ruffs you need three entries to dummy: the ◇A, the ♠A and the ♣K.

If you have made your plan, turn over to see the full deal:

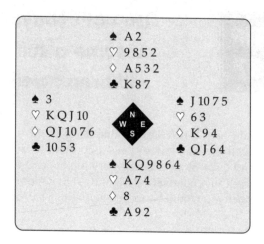

```
              ♠ A 2
              ♡ 9 8 5 2
              ◇ A 5 3 2
              ♣ K 8 7
♠ 3                        ♠ J 10 7 5
♡ K Q J 10      N          ♡ 6 3
◇ Q J 10 7 6  W   E        ◇ K 9 4
♣ 10 5 3        S          ♣ Q J 6 4
              ♠ K Q 9 8 6 4
              ♡ A 7 4
              ◇ 8
              ♣ A 9 2
```

Duck the ♡K lead as that may enable you to find out how the suit breaks. West continues with the ♡Q. You have seen East play the ♡6 and then the ♡3; this suggests that he has a doubleton and therefore that the suit breaks 4-2 and will not supply another trick.

What most players would do now is to cross to the ♠A and then follow with a second trump to the king; they discover the bad trump break too late: their third entry (the ♣A) has been used up.

You should plan for the bad break: after winning the ♡A, take the ◇A and ruff a diamond, then play trumps in a slightly odd order: the ♠K then ♠A. Now, if the trumps break normally, then you can cross to the ♣A and finish drawing them; and if trumps break badly, you are in the right hand to ruff a second diamond. Finally you cash the ♠Q, the ♣A, the ♣K and then play the fourth diamond. East is helpless: if he ruffs with the jack, you will make your trump later, and if he discards, then your ruff is your tenth trick.

It takes a lot of planning, but it is worth it: trumps will break 4-1 more than a quarter of the time and since the contract would have been easy if they had broken evenly, it gave you something to think about!

Whenever things look too easy, try to spend some of your thinking time at trick one working out what might go wrong and making a plan to cope with it.

Drop a high card to put off the defence

Quite often in a suit contract you will have that sinking feeling when an opponent leads an ace in a suit where you have three in dummy and three in your hand: after the ace and king, a ruff will follow and down your contract goes. You may just be able to put the defence off track by dropping a high card on the first trick; after all, how can the leader be sure that it is his partner who has the shorter holding?

For example:

West leads the ♡A against 4♠, dummy follows with the four and East plays the two. If South follows with the six or eight, West is sure to play his king next and get the good news; eventually giving his partner a ruff on the third round. However, if South follows with the ♡Q how does West know what to do?

The layout could be:

Now if West continues with the ♡K, it will be ruffed and dummy's jack will be established.

There are many examples of this kind of play, but by far the most common ones are those at trick one and it is worth being aware of them because they can make a huge difference to a deal. Take this one, for example:

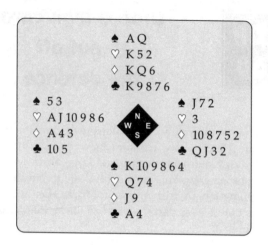

♠ A Q	
♡ K 5 2	
◊ K Q 6	
♣ K 9 8 7 6	

♠ 5 3	♠ J 7 2
♡ A J 10 9 8 6	♡ 3
◊ A 4 3	◊ 10 8 7 5 2
♣ 10 5	♣ Q J 3 2

♠ K 10 9 8 6 4
♡ Q 7 4
◊ J 9
♣ A 4

West	North	East	South
2♡[1]	2NT	Pass	4♠
All Pass			

[1] Weak Two, 6-10 points, six-card suit

Against 4♠ by South, West leads the ♡A.

I have given you the full layout because I am sure you have guessed what you need to do!

West has made a speculative lead; expecting the heart strength to be on his left for the 2NT bid, he is hoping to find his partner with shortage. Unfortunately for you the lead is likely to be a spectacular success; he will be able to continue with a heart for his partner to ruff and if he has the ◊A, he will be able to win that and give his partner a second ruff. 4♠ minus one will not look good on the score-card.

Try the effect of dropping the ♡Q underneath the ♡A lead. Now West will perhaps think that *you* have the shortage in hearts and play a club before you discard one on the ♡K. You can win the club switch and draw trumps, claiming eleven tricks: 4♠ plus one – quite a contrast.

West might see through your deception, but if you play the ♡Q in tempo, it will not be easy for him.

Whenever you think a defender has stumbled on a line of play which will defeat your contract, try to find a way to make him walk away from it. Once again, it pays to plan before playing from dummy at trick one; then once your thinking is done you will be able to follow smoothly from hand with your high honour, in the hope that your opponent will be successfully duped.

Play your highest card to tempt a defender to cover

There is a lot of psychology in bridge. In theory it should make no difference which card you lead: your opponent should think soundly about the situation and come up with the right answer. However, there are many players who will happily put a king on a queen, but would be less keen to cover a ten with a king. Why this should be so, I cannot tell you, but perhaps it is the prevalence of the old rules that echo in our minds about covering honours. The ten always seems so much smaller than the queen and thus it does not tempt us into covering.

How can you use this to your advantage?

Sometimes you will want your opponent to cover and sometimes you will not – thus you can choose which card to lead in order to get the desired result. For example:

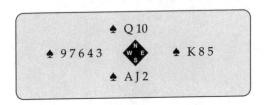

You have no entries to the South hand other than in spades, but you would like to make three tricks in the suit if you can. The problem is that there is a blockage: if you lead the ♠Q, East is likely to cover it, leaving you with the ♠10 and ♠J as winners, but you cannot reach the jack since there are no entries. However, you might try leading the ♠10 to start with: East may duck this and then you can follow with the queen; if East now covers, this play will give you three spade tricks. Clearly East should not allow you to make three tricks, but things are not always so easy when you are at the table.

The most common occasion when you want a player to cover is when you have a two-way finesse:

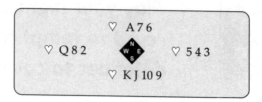

```
             ♡ A 7 6
♡ Q 8 2        N           ♡ 5 4 3
            W     E
               S
             ♡ K J 10 9
```

South can take the finesse in hearts either way; a clever way of giving yourself an extra chance is to start by leading the ♡J from the South hand. A lot of Wests will fall into the trap and cover the jack with their queen and now you make all four tricks in the suit. If West ducks smoothly then you would win with North's ace and take a finesse through East. If this finesse loses to West's queen, then you should congratulate West on his good defence. Ducking smoothly when right-hand opponent leads an honour is not easy; you have to plan carefully for it.

Here are two similar deals: one in which you want your opponents to win the first trick, the other, where you would prefer them not to:

```
♠ K 3
♡ K 5 3
◇ J 8 6
♣ K J 8 7 6

      N
   W     E
      S

♠ Q J 2
♡ A Q 4 2
◇ 4 3
♣ A Q 3 2
```

The contract is 3NT by South; the lead is the ♠10.

Play small from dummy and, if all goes well, East (holding the ace) will let the lead run to your queen. Having avoided a diamond switch, you can take nine tricks.

The second deal is:

♠ K 3
♡ K 5 3
◇ J 8 6
♣ K 10 8 7 6

♠ Q J 2
♡ A 7 4 2
◇ A 4
♣ Q J 3 2

The contract: 3NT by South; lead: ♠10.

This time you would prefer East to take his ace and continue the suit, so leap up with the ♠K. East will probably take his ace and return the suit. You win the queen and knock out the ♣A, making nine tricks in comfort.

If you play low on the opening lead, your queen will win the first trick, but you will still need to knock out two aces and if the defence switch to diamonds they may well defeat you.

When you defend, I am sure you would not be fooled by such simple tactics, but remember that defence is a tremendously difficult part of the game and the more pressure you heap on the defenders, the more likely they are to make a mistake.

Draw trumps first unless you have a good reason not to

TIP 40

Basically, the quicker you draw trumps the better, because then there is no danger of an opponent's ruff. However, there are three main reasons for not drawing trumps:

1. You need a ruff in the short hand.
2. You need to use your trumps as entries for a long suit.
3. You have losers to deal with, before you can lose a trump trick.

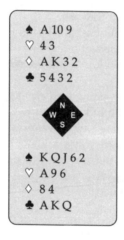

```
    ♠ A 10 9
    ♡ 4 3
    ◇ A K 3 2
    ♣ 5 4 3 2
         N
       W   E
         S
    ♠ K Q J 6 2
    ♡ A 9 6
    ◇ 8 4
    ♣ A K Q
```

You are the declarer in 6♠, with no opposition bidding. How do you play on the ♡K lead?

Slam hands are easier to plan if you look at one hand and consider its losers. Take the South hand: there are no losers in spades, two possible losers in hearts, the two little diamonds are covered by dummy's ace-king, and there are no losers in clubs either.

So your plan is to get rid of one of your heart losers. With that decided, you should see the opportunity of ruffing one in dummy – but if you draw trumps you will have no trumps to trump with! Hence you should play hearts right away, take your ruff and then draw trumps.

You let the ♡K hold the trick and win the continuation; then ruff your last heart, and that's it: your last loser has disappeared, and therefore it is time to draw trumps as soon as possible.

Here is a deal demonstrating the second theme:

♠ A 10 9
♡ 4 3
◇ K Q J 10
♣ 5 4 3 2

♠ K Q J 6 2
♡ A K
◇ 8 4
♣ A K 8 7

You are in 6♠ again, but this time the lead is the ♡Q.

Again, focusing on the South hand, you can see that there are no spade losers, no heart losers, one diamond loser and two possible club losers. How can you get rid of these losers?

The ◇A has to be lost, but with three diamond winners in dummy, the two little clubs can be discarded. Be careful not to end your plan there, for you should always consider whether you have the entries to carry out your plan. Say you draw trumps and then play diamonds, can you see the problem now? The defenders will take their ◇A on the second round and your diamonds will be stranded.

As long as you work this out at trick one, you will realise that you need a trump as an entry. Therefore you win the ♡A, draw just two round of trumps and then play diamonds; once you have knocked out the ◇A, then you can draw the last round of trumps, finishing in dummy, allowing you to discard the little clubs.

Whenever you have a long suit which needs establishing in a suit contract, check the entry situation carefully. One way of doing this is to take away the trumps from the hand and see if there are any entries left; that would certainly have helped you here. It is amazing how quickly entries can disappear if you do not look after them carefully.

The technique of playing a long suit before drawing trumps is quite a common one and although it might appear dangerous, it is often very necessary.

The next deal takes us on to the last theme, that of discarding losers quickly; this tends to be important if there is a chance that there might be a trump loser and thus that the defence might get the lead quite soon. How would you tackle 6♠ from the South seat, after winning the ♡K lead with your ace?

```
       ♠ 10 8 4
       ♡ 4 3
       ◊ A K Q 2
       ♣ 5 4 3 2
            N
         W     E
            S
       ♠ K Q J 9 6 2
       ♡ A 9 6
       ◊ 8
       ♣ A K Q
```

From the South hand, you have one spade loser and two possible heart losers. The hearts are easily disposed of, on the top diamonds, so there should be little difficulty. However, because you have to lose a trick in trumps, you cannot afford to play the trumps first: the defence will win the ♠A and cash a heart trick. With the lead hitting your weak spot, you need to discard those hearts right away, so you win the ♡A and play out the ◊A-K-Q. With the hearts discarded, you can set about drawing trumps.

You have seen three deals where you should not draw trumps first, but in each case we formulated a plan and found an excellent reason for not drawing them. However, in the majority of cases drawing trumps is the best policy. If you cannot think of a good reason not to, then draw trumps.

Do not waste your trumps

You should almost always avoid "wasting" your long trumps by ruffing unless forced to use them by your opponents. It can be so tempting to ruff when you have a singleton in your hand, but unless you have a very good reason, you should resist the temptation: you may well need those trumps later on.

Consider this example:

♠ A 9
♡ J 10 2
◇ A 5 3 2
♣ 9 8 7 6

♠ K Q 8 6 4 2
♡ A K
◇ 8
♣ Q J 10 2

Here is a 4♠ contract against which West leads the ◇Q.

You have no reason to ruff a diamond – in fact it would be fatal as the cards lie. You do not gain a trick by ruffing in the long hand: your six likely trump tricks will always be there whether you ruff or not. "Surely it makes no difference?" you might say.

Consider how the play may progress after you ruff a diamond: you win the ◇A at trick one, ruff a diamond and start drawing trumps, but after the ♠A and the ♠K, you see East discard. Can you see the problem? You are down to three trumps (Q-8-6), whilst West still has two left (J-10). It looks OK, but since you still have to lose the lead twice in clubs, your opponents will continue leading diamonds to "force" your trumps. You will have to admit defeat, since the complete deal is:

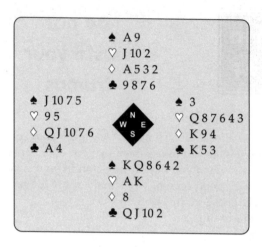

Can you see how you brought about your own downfall? You started the defence's job for them. When trumps break badly, the defence's aim is to attack declarer's trumps in order to force him to lose control. They attacked the right suit and their plan was to continue diamonds at every opportunity. However, as long as you do not help them, you will eventually prevail.

You win the ◇A, draw three rounds of trumps leaving the ♠J outstanding (see Tip 42) and then knock out the clubs. East wins the ♣K and plays a diamond, but you are one step ahead now, with the extra trump that you need to retain control. You ruff the diamond and still have two trumps left, so you can knock out the ♣A safely. West can cash his trump winner, but you still have control and can claim your contract.

Trumps are precious, so unless you have good reasons do not waste trumps in the long hand.

Consider leaving a lone defensive trump winner out

When the opponents have just one trump left, it will take two of your trumps to draw it. This will often be worth it, if it is a small trump, as you thus prevent the defence from using it for ruffing. However, if that lone trump is a winner, then it will always make whether they ruff with it or not and you should prefer not to waste two of your trumps on it.

Below is a trump suit which is often suitable for this type of play:

♠ A K 4 3   ♠ 10 7 5 2

You cash the ace-king and leave the fifth defensive trump outstanding because it is a winner. Meanwhile you might be able to use your remaining small trumps for ruffing.

Even if you only need to waste one trump to get rid of the defence's top trump, it will often be best to leave it out – especially when you have other things to do (e.g. establish tricks or take a finesse). Here is a deal that illustrates this point; the contract is 4♠ by South on the ♣Q lead and you have to deal with a 4-1 trump break:

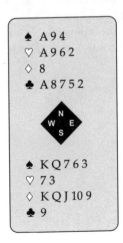

♠ A 9 4
♡ A 9 6 2
◇ 8
♣ A 8 7 5 2

♠ K Q 7 6 3
♡ 7 3
◇ K Q J 10 9
♣ 9

You win the ♣A and start drawing trumps (you have no need to ruff diamonds in dummy) by playing the ♠A and the ♠K. Unfortunately West discards on this, but you press on with the ♠Q. East now has one trump left, but it is the top one. Do not draw this last trump, even though it only costs you one trump to do it – you have other matters to deal with. Knock out the ◇A and let East take his trump when he wants; you still have one extra trump and with the ◇A gone your hand has enough winners for you to prevail.

The full deal is illustrated in the diagram below:

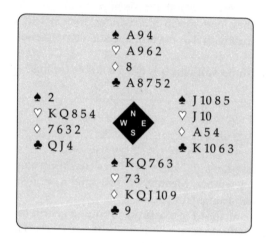

Notice what happens if you do draw the fourth round of trumps: East wins and plays a club, which forces your last trump. Now when you knock out the ◇A, not only can East cash two club winners, but you cannot reach your diamond winners!

Leaving a top trump outstanding allows you to conserve your trumps and also helps you keep control of the hand.

DEFENCE TIPS

Keep four-card suits intact whenever possible

A four-card suit is a very valuable thing – bear that in mind when contemplating your discards. So often a discard from such a suit will cost a trick because declarer also has four cards there. If you acquire the habit of keeping your four-card suits intact, you will become a much better defender. Look at this suit, as an extreme example:

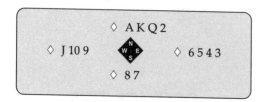

East's diamonds look worthless but because there are four of them, they will outlast West's and South's higher cards: the six will beat North's two on the last round. However, one discard from East and North's two would become a winner.

Now consider this defensive problem:

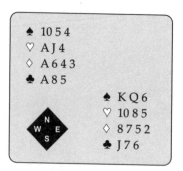

The auction is brief: 1NT (12-14) by South – 3NT by North. Your partner, West, leads the ♠7 to your queen which holds the trick, but when you lead the king declarer's ace wins. Partner appears to have started with five spades to the jack. Declarer plays out four rounds of hearts; what do you discard?

A better question would be: what *don't* you discard?

The answer, of course, is that you must *not* discard a diamond:

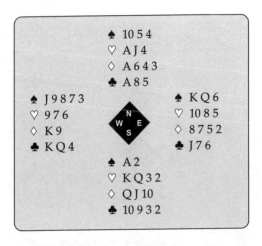

Declarer has an easy nine tricks when the diamond finesse works: four hearts, three diamonds and two aces, but note that if you lazily throw a diamond away, nine tricks will become ten. The ace, king, queen, jack, ten and nine go on the first three rounds of diamonds, so as long as you still have the eight you should win the final round.

Here is another example:

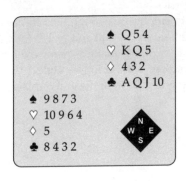

West	North	East	South
		3◊	3NT
Pass	6NT	All Pass	

You lead your partner's suit and declarer ducks your partner's eight, but then wins with his ace on the next round; what do you discard?

You have three four-card suits this time, but you can see that one is useless – clubs – because dummy's suit can beat every one of your cards; thus you discard a club and that is the last worry you should have, for the full deal is:

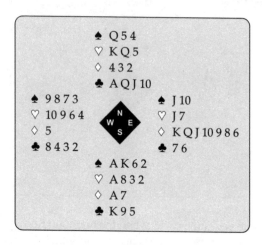

When declarer leads dummy's clubs, you are in a position of power because you discard after declarer; and generally in situations like this you should discard the same suit as declarer. As you can see, declarer actually has both four-card majors, so that a careless discard in either would have cost a trick.

It is impossible to emphasise enough how important your four-card suits are. If in doubt, save your suit and search for another discard. You will find that declarers do not make as many overtricks against you as they used to, since they will no longer collect those extra tricks that careless discarding gifted them at the end of play.

Tips for Better Bridge

Give count on declarer's leads

Distribution signals are very important in defence because if you know how many cards your partner has in a suit, you can work out how many declarer has, which means that you can defend accurately.

♣ K Q J 10 4

♣ A 9 3

Declarer starts leading his club suit from dummy. Dummy has no outside entries, so it is your job to cut declarer off; when do you take your ace?

It depends on which card your partner plays on the first club. Your partner will give you a count signal (whenever declarer leads it is good to get in to the habit of giving a count signal) as follows:

High – low shows an even number of cards
Low – high shows an odd number of cards

You will have used a high-low signal to show a doubleton; the principle here is the same, so when you see a high-low signal, you will know that partner has two or four cards (or even six). When you see partner following up the line, he will have three or five cards.

Let's go back to the question above, but let's answer it in two different situations:

1. when declarer leads the ♣K, partner follows with ♣7; and
2. when declarer leads the ♣K, partner follows with ♣2.

How do you play in each case?

In case (i) your partner is trying to show an even number of clubs, most likely a doubleton; so adding up around the table: five in dummy, three in your hand and two in partner's hand leaves (13-10) = three in declarer's hand. Therefore you would duck two rounds of clubs and win the third round. The full layout of the suit is shown on the next page:

However, in case (ii) partner is suggesting an odd number of cards (following low), therefore the sums are slightly different: 5+3+3 = 11, leaving declarer with just two, so you would win your ace on the second round. This time the layout would be:

This kind of play comes up on almost every deal and it is important to be accurate. If West ducks an extra round in case (ii), he gives declarer an extra trick. Remember that he has no entry to get back to dummy, so he should only be able to make one club trick.

Let's look at the tip in the context of a full deal:

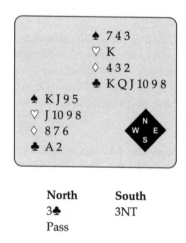

North	South
3♣	3NT
Pass	

Once again a swift auction, and you choose the ♡J as your lead. Dummy's ♡K wins and declarer immediately advances the ♣K; what do you do?

Your immediate reaction is probably to duck, but the answer depends on partner's signal. Your partner followed with the ♣6.

With the 10-9-8 in dummy, there is no doubt that this is a high card (almost the highest partner could play); this means partner has an even number of clubs: two or four.

Doing your calculations, this leaves declarer with one or three. If declarer has three, it doesn't matter what you do, since whether you win the first or second club declarer will still have a club left to reach dummy. So you should concentrate on the number that does matter – one – and you should take the first club:

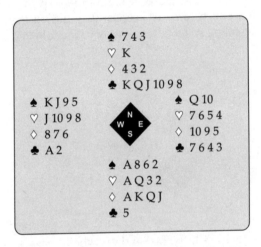

Declarer has eight top tricks and if you deny him a club trick, he will go down. Duck just once and declarer will be home and dry.

South would certainly have been better off in clubs, but it is never easy to bid a 20-point hand after your partner has pre-empted.

Count signals are very important. So often it will be the weaker hand (here, East) who is able to help out the stronger hand by giving information about suit length, thereby allowing the partnership to visualise declarer's hand and defend accordingly.

Keep the right cards rather than signal

Making a wonderful signal and having a partner respond to it, might make a difference on one in fifty deals, but keeping the right cards will make a difference on one in two. The difference in importance really is that marked: if defenders spent as much time thinking about which cards to keep as they did on their weird and wonderful signalling systems, they would be much better at defending!

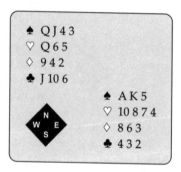

South opens 1NT (15-17 points) and everybody passes. Your partner finds the right lead for a change and proceeds to take the first four diamond tricks: ◊A-K-Q-J. Everybody followed to the first three rounds, but now it is time for a discard.

Before you make your decision I should tell you that you are playing McKenney (also called "Lavinthal") discards: a high discard would ask for the higher-ranking outstanding suit, a low discard would ask for a lower-ranking outstanding suit.

Many Easts would reason that they want a spade lead, so they would signal for a spade – unfortunately, to do that, they would have to throw a high card which would mean letting go of a heart as the clubs are too small.

It will be no surprise to you, having read Tip 43, that the heart discard gives declarer his contract.

It is much more important to keep the right cards than to signal. Throw away a club: you are not that worried about a spade switch,

---

Tips for Better Bridge

since your ♠A-K are likely to make anyway, but you are worried about you precious four-card heart suit.

The full deal is:

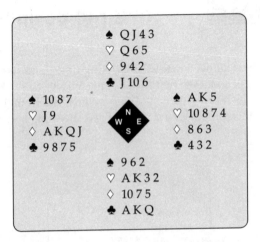

```
                    ♠ Q J 4 3
                    ♡ Q 6 5
                    ◇ 9 4 2
                    ♣ J 10 6
    ♠ 10 8 7                        ♠ A K 5
    ♡ J 9            N              ♡ 10 8 7 4
    ◇ A K Q J      W   E            ◇ 8 6 3
    ♣ 9 8 7 5        S              ♣ 4 3 2
                    ♠ 9 6 2
                    ♡ A K 3 2
                    ◇ 10 7 5
                    ♣ A K Q
```

There is nothing wrong with having a discarding system, but keeping the right cards is paramount. As you can see, both sides have six tricks and it is a struggle to make a seventh. As long as you keep all your hearts you should win the struggle, so that if declarer played his three winning clubs, you would then discard the ♠5, still keeping your hearts intact.

Signals are wonderful when they work and we can dine out on them, discussing how successful they were. However, such triumphs are all too rare. Just think how many stories declarers can tell about defenders who threw the wrong card!

Take your time
when dummy
is put down

Everybody is allowed extended thinking-time on the first trick, not just to think about the first trick but to envisage the whole defence. Try to plan which card you would play on any lead from dummy; that way, you will be prepared and will not give anything away.

For example:

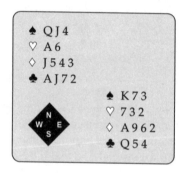

```
              ♠ Q J 4
              ♡ A 6
              ◊ J 5 4 3
              ♣ A J 7 2
                              ♠ K 7 3
                              ♡ 7 3 2
                              ◊ A 9 6 2
                              ♣ Q 5 4
```

West	North	East	South
			1NT[1]
Pass	3NT	All Pass	
[1]12-14			

You are East defending against 3NT. Your partner leads the ♡Q and declarer wins in dummy with the ace. Plan your defence.

Do not let declarer's quick play of the ♡A put you off; the rules (Law 73 in the *White Book*, the EBU's Tournament Directors' Guide) specifically allow you extra thinking-time on the first trick. There is a lot to take in when dummy is laid down. What you should be thinking about is which card you might play in any of the four suits. Ask yourself questions such as: "Would I cover the ♠Q or the ♣J?" If you answer these questions before the relevant cards are led, you will be in a position to follow smoothly with whichever card you have chosen, giving declarer no hints as to your holdings. By looking at each suit in turn like this, you will also tune your mind to the likely plays that will occur and will thus be more likely to find any winning line of defence.

Too many defenders would have followed with the ♡2 as soon as declarer had played his ace and then would have been stopped in their tracks when dummy played the ♣J.

It is crucial that you follow low smoothly to the ♣J, but this is only possible if you have thought about it before, otherwise surely you will be put on the spot.

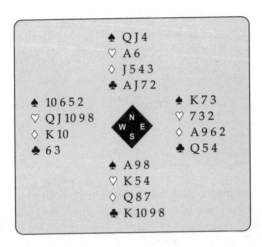

Declarer has made a clever play. By playing quickly from dummy and hopefully inducing you to follow quickly, he can then play the ♣J and see your response: if you follow smoothly, he will assume that you do not have the ♣Q, and will therefore win the ♣K and take the finesse against your partner. However, if you stop to think he will know you have the queen and will capture it easily.

By taking your time at trick one you can prepare yourself for the unexpected and therefore avoid giving declarer any clues.

High cards
are for killing
other high cards

This is a simple but very important tip. If you can make your high cards work harder in defence, you will find yourself doing so much better. Here is a suit featured in Tip 36:

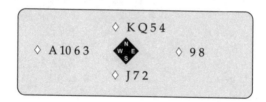

Playing in no-trumps, declarer is trying to make three tricks in this diamond suit. He does best to lead up to his double-honour holding. However, so long as West is patient, his ace can eventually kill an honour.

The first trick goes: ◊2, ◊3, ◊K, ◊9.
Declarer then returns to hand and the second trick goes:
◊7, ◊6, ◊Q, ◊8.

Finally West is able to win the last two diamonds. If, however, he plays his ace on either of the first two rounds, it will be wasted – winning the trick, but not killing an honour.
  Here is another layout:

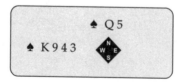

South leads the ♠2 in a no-trump contract.
  Your king's job is to kill an honour, so you should follow small. Here is the full suit layout:

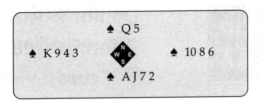

Your king's aim is to kill the jack and by waiting for a later round it will be able to fulfil that purpose.

This is a defensive situation that many players find difficult:

Declarer leads the ♡10.

If declarer has the ♡Q your king is going to die whatever you do, but what if your partner holds the queen? Generally your honours are only able to kill high cards on their right: for instance, your king cannot kill dummy's jack because declarer can lead up to it. This is the key: if you let the ♡10 run to your partner's queen, your king will not be able to do its work. Your king's job is to kill the ten, so you must cover it. A look at the full suit will help to see how this works:

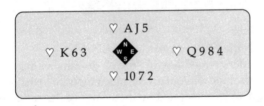

Declarer has little hope of making more than one trick in this suit if he leads it himself (he needs West to hold the king and queen, or he needs West to have a doubleton honour; his correct lead should be a small heart). However, it is surprising how often the ten will be allowed to run to the queen, leaving a simple finesse against the king and two tricks for declarer. If the king kills the ten then, although the ace can take the first trick, East's Q-9 is now sitting over dummy's jack.

There will be occasions where you have to play your honours on thin air, but try your hardest to make sure that this does not happen often.

Do not waste intermediate cards

Take a look at this suit:

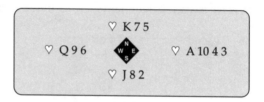

If declarer plays the suit himself, he will lose three tricks. Perhaps hoping for a little luck towards the end of play, he may lead towards dummy's king hoping West has the ace, but the king would lose to the ace and South's jack would then be scythed by West's queen.

However, put yourself in West's shoes:

Declarer leads the ♡2; what do you play?

Some defenders would like to "force" dummy's king and therefore would insert the nine without giving much thought to the consequences. That's a mistake, as illustrated by the layout of the suit after trick one has been played:

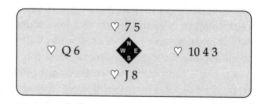

The ace and king went along with West's nine on the first trick; now it is East's ten that is trapped between South's J-8 and declarer can make a trick.

As a defender, it is important to remember that declarer cannot see your cards. Very rarely do you need to force cards out, because declarer is going to play that card anyway. With this suit there was no doubt that declarer was going to play the king whichever card you played – after all a deep finesse of the seven would be rather strange nor would it help declarer's cause!

Here is another situation where it is important to play low smoothly:

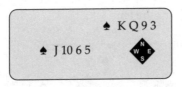

Declarer leads the ♠2.

As before, you have to remember that declarer cannot actually see your hand; he has no idea that you hold the ♠J-10 and since it is heavily against the odds that you do hold both those cards, he is unlikely to play you for them. The full suit layout is:

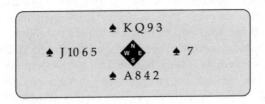

You follow low smoothly and declarer plays the ♠K as expected, and now your spade trick is guaranteed. If you do "waste" one of your jack-ten on the first round, then if declarer guesses that you started with length in the suit he can cash the ♠A and finesse your second honour to take all four tricks. Of course if declarer had played the nine from dummy on the first round after you had followed low, he would have won the trick, but how would he know what you hold?

One last example:

Declarer leads the ♣2 in a no-trump contract.

Once again you should play low smoothly. A good declarer will know that it is more likely that the king and queen are split between the two hands, and so may well play the nine from dummy on the first trick, hoping West has the ten:

As you can see, if you duck the first trick and declarer plays the nine, you will make two tricks. However, if you play your king or queen on the first round, declarer should manage to lose just one trick.

If you find that every time you play low in situations like those described above, your opponent tends to play the right card and you feel that you have lost out, there maybe a very simple solution to your problems: hold your cards up higher! I mean this genuinely, for quite often it will be the case that an opponent – through no fault of his own nor with any intent to try to peek – will catch a glimpse of your cards because they are held too low down.

Assuming declarer cannot see your cards, then try to stick to the rule of "Second hand plays low"; it can be right to play high second in hand, but only very rarely.

Pick two key suits to concentrate on during the play

Concentrating on all the fifty-two cards on every deal is very difficult and beyond most of us, so I recommend that you try to pick two suits that you think will be important for your defence. You are more likely to be able to focus on half the pack, and once you have chosen the key suits you will take more notice of discards in those suits and have a better chance of working out what is going on. Thinking about those suits early, and trying to analyse them, will very often save a guess at the end. For example:

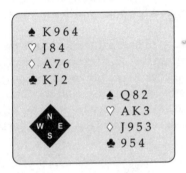

	♠ K 9 6 4		
	♡ J 8 4		
	◇ A 7 6		
	♣ K J 2		

♠ Q 8 2
♡ A K 3
◇ J 9 5 3
♣ 9 5 4

West	North	East	South
			1NT
Pass	2♣	Pass	2◇
Pass	3NT	All Pass	

South opened a weak no-trump (12-14 points); North used Stayman and then raised to 3NT. With his flat hand, North may have done better not to bother with Stayman in the first place.

You are East defending against 3NT; your partner leads the ♡10.

Before you get going, which are the key suits for you?

Spades and diamonds.

Hearts will soon be gone; indeed, your partner takes the ♡Q on the third round and then cashes the thirteenth heart.

Both diamonds and spades might be important. What do we know from the bidding?

South does not have four spades (remember the 2◇ response to Stayman), which means partner has at least three. Assuming declarer has the ♠A (otherwise partner could take declarer down now!) what happens if declarer also has the ♠J?

Declarer would be able to take a simple finesse in spades, so it looks as if you are going to need some help from your partner in spades.

What about diamonds? Well, if declarer has four diamonds, you need to keep your diamonds because your partner will only have two and thus will be unable to help.

Why all this thought?

Because so often in these type of contracts, after you have taken the first four tricks, declarer will start running tricks and you will have to decide which cards to keep. At the end of play you will find that you may not be able to guard both spades and diamonds: you will have to decide which to keep. Almost always in this type of situation the defenders need to work together: they have to guard one suit each, so what you are trying to work out is which suit you should guard. Watch as the play unfolds:

On the fourth round of hearts dummy throws the ◇6, you throw the ♣4 and declarer throws the ◇2. Keep in mind these diamond discards.

Your partner switches to a club and now the action starts, for it appears that declarer has four easy club tricks and he starts playing them off: he wins the ♣K-J and then leads the ♣2 to his queen, at which point you have to make your next discard and the layout is:

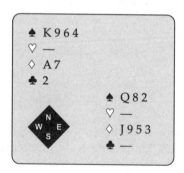

Declarer has four clubs, so he could not have started with five diamonds. Note also that he has discarded a diamond, so you can afford a diamond discard because declarer does not have four left. You discard the ◇3. It is no surprise to see the ♣A come next and now it is time for the crucial discard. However, it should be no problem for you because you had already done the hard work: you need help from your partner in spades and he needs your help in diamonds, i.e. you look after diamonds and he looks after spades. Thus you discard a spade and declarer has to lose a trick at the end, for the full deal is:

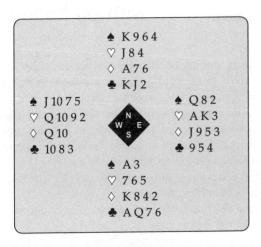

♠ K 9 6 4
♡ J 8 4
♢ A 7 6
♣ K J 2

♠ J 10 7 5
♡ Q 10 9 2
♢ Q 10
♣ 10 8 3

♠ Q 8 2
♡ A K 3
♢ J 9 5 3
♣ 9 5 4

♠ A 3
♡ 7 6 5
♢ K 8 4 2
♣ A Q 7 6

That is a very difficult defence and the only chance of avoiding a guess is by thinking things through early. Focusing on two suits will give you a chance to try to evaluate all the available information. How often do you find yourself with the unenviable task of choosing your discard in the last stages of the play, knowing that if you make a mistake declarer will make his game? Here you were the only defender who could look after diamonds because your partner's two cards fall under the ace and king but your partner, holding length in spades, was able to take care of the spades for you. Had you discarded a second diamond at the end, declarer's third diamond would have been a winner and his contract would have been made.

Great defence is a partnership exercise and almost always each of you has to take responsibility for just one suit – working out which is which is the difficult part! Your best chance of avoiding a guess is by thinking about the key suits early.

If in doubt, cover an honour with an honour

There is much to think about when an honour is led on your right and if possible you should work out whether it is right or wrong to cover. If you cannot work it out, then cover, because it is usually the right thing to do. This is because your aim is to promote a trick for yourself or your partner, and also, as seen in previous tips, you want to use your honours to kill honours in declarer's or dummy's hands.

The main reasons *not* to cover an honour are:

1. if the lead is from two touching honours (see Tip 51);
2. when there is nothing to gain; and
3. when your holding is long enough to avoid capture.

Let us look at some examples:

South leads the ♡10. What do you do?

You have seen this example before (Tip 48), but it merits a second showing. Unless you have thought of a very good reason not to, you should cover the ten – it is your king's job to kill it:

Once your king has killed the ten, your partner's queen will be ready for dummy's jack and you will keep declarer down to one trick in the suit. If you fail to cover, then after partner's queen wins the first trick, declarer will make the next two with a simple finesse. Honours can only kill the cards on their right – it is important to keep that in mind.

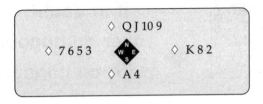

Dummy leads the ◇Q. Do you cover or not?

This suit shows a situation when you should not cover (point 2: when there is nothing to gain). The tip says cover if in doubt, but with dummy holding such a solid suit surely there can be no doubts: there is no chance for a promotion and, since declarer only has two diamonds in his hand, after the queen wins the first trick he has to play the ace on the second, leaving your king as the master for the third round.

The next example looks similar, but be careful how you play:

Declarer leads the ♠10 from his hand; what should you do?

This is where the tip can come in handy: if unsure of what to do, you should cover and your partner will be glad because the full lay-out is:

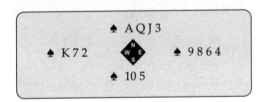

Dummy's suit is not completely solid and if your partner has four cards he is bound to be able to beat the fourth card in dummy. It is so important that your king kills the ten, for as I mentioned before it can only kill the honours on its right. A cover promotes your partner's nine to win the fourth round, but if you duck, declarer's ten wins the first trick and then he leads a second spade to his jack and dummy's ace will then bring down your king, for four easy tricks.

To finish, let us look at point 3, when you have enough length to protect your honour from the finesse:

Dummy leads the ♣Q and you have a choice: if you suspect that declarer has length in the suit, you should duck; but if you think declarer is short you should cover to try to promote partner's ten. So, if the layout is as in the next diagram:

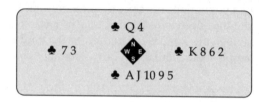

When declarer is trying to establish the suit, you can protect your king by ducking, so the queen wins the first trick and the jack can win the next, but with no more cards in dummy declarer cannot finesse again, so all he can do is win his ace and give you the fourth trick. If you had covered, of course, declarer could have run the suit.

However, consider the layout below:

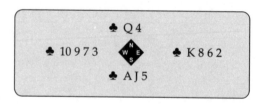

If you think declarer is short, it is important to cover, so that you only allow declarer to make two tricks: the queen, king and ace go on the first trick and declarer can win his jack on the second, but your partner's ten can win the third round. If you do not cover, then declarer makes three tricks: the queen wins the first and then a simple finesse will give him the next two.

As you can see, deciding whether to cover is not easy, but if you cannot work out exactly what to do, then I recommend covering, because in the long run it is right more often than not.

TIP 51

If a lead is from two honours, it is best not to cover

The full rule usually reads: "If you can equally well cover a second honour, then wait and cover the second honour."

Most players are familiar with this rule, so when a queen is led from queen-jack they withhold their king, but they are not so familiar with the idea of withholding their ace when a king is led from king-queen. If you can duck smoothly, you can obtain some great results – and, once again, deciding on your play before the lead is made will allow you to play in tempo and also, with luck, fool the declarer. For example:

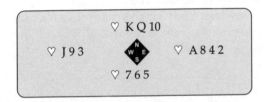

Declarer leads the ♡5 and plays the king from dummy; if you win the ace, then declarer will finesse your partner's jack on the next round and make two easy tricks. However, if you duck smoothly on the first round, you give declarer a dilemma: from his point of view it probably looks as if West has the ace, so he may well lead towards dummy again and put up the queen, assuming that it will win. That will not be the case, as you will kill it with your ace and your partner will then be able to take the third trick with his jack.

It is often not obvious why this rule works. Intuitively it would seem that there is little difference between covering the first and the second honour, but let me assure you that the rule is well worth following even if you cannot grasp it! Basically, if you cover the first honour you will often expose your partner to a finesse, as in the example above (West's jack was within the jaws of dummy's queen-ten) and the same is also true in the following example of a the queen-jack holding:

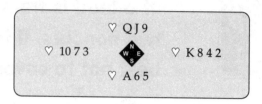

♡ QJ9

♡ 10 7 3   ♡ K 8 4 2

♡ A 6 5

The queen is led from dummy and if you cover with your king then declarer can win his ace and finesse for your partner's ten on the next round, scoring three tricks. However, if you duck, then although the queen wins the first trick, declarer cannot engineer a third trick: if he leads the jack you cover and promote partner's ten, and if he plays small then you duck and declarer's ace cannot kill your king.

If the reasons behind when to cover and when not to cover are not apparent to you, then stick to the rule: when the lead is from two honours, do not cover the first lead.

Generally if declarer leads a high honour from his hand, you should assume he also has the card beneath it (if it is not in dummy) and therefore you should duck:

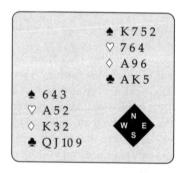

♠ K 7 5 2
♡ 7 6 4
◇ A 9 6
♣ A K 5

♠ 6 4 3
♡ A 5 2
◇ K 3 2
♣ Q J 10 9

South opened with a weak no-trump (12-14) and North jumped to 3NT. The ♣Q lead from your hand is fairly automatic. What are your thoughts when you see dummy?

Look at your high cards; when are you going to play them? Are you ready?

Declarer wins the ♣A and leads a heart to his king, which you duck smoothly having already planned your play. Declarer then follows with the ◇Q, which again you duck smoothly, allowing it to win. After some thought, declarer plays a small diamond to the ace and plays another heart to his queen. The full deal is:

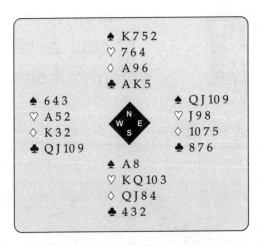

♠ K 7 5 2
♡ 7 6 4
◇ A 9 6
♣ A K 5

♠ 6 4 3
♡ A 5 2
◇ K 3 2
♣ Q J 10 9

♠ Q J 10 9
♡ J 9 8
◇ 10 7 5
♣ 8 7 6

♠ A 8
♡ K Q 10 3
◇ Q J 8 4
♣ 4 3 2

Brilliant! You have fooled declarer by thinking ahead and being in a position to play smoothly whichever card he played. He placed East with the ♡A, so when he played his second heart from dummy he expected his queen to make, but you kill it with your ace and knock out the last club stop. You have five defensive tricks: two clubs, the ◇K, the ♡A and the ♡J.

Covering honours is a difficult area, but remember that when you think that there are two honours together, then you must not cover the first led.

Keep your honour to kill dummy's honour

If there is an honour in dummy and you have an honour sitting over it, then you should try to keep your honour to kill dummy's honour, even if that means you have to play low on your partner's lead:

♡ Q 10 8

♡ K 7 6

Your partner leads the ♡2 against 4♠. Dummy plays the ♡8. What do you play?

You know that your partner does not have the ♡A because he would not underlead an ace against a suit contract (see Tip 55). That means that if you play your king it will be killed by declarer's ace, and then an obvious finesse could be taken against your partner – three tricks to declarer. Keep your king to kill dummy's queen: play low.

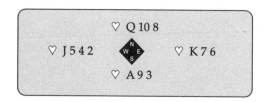

♡ Q 10 8

♡ J 5 4 2   ♡ K 7 6

♡ A 9 3

Declarer wins the first trick with the ♡8, but cannot now make all three tricks as long as the defenders do not lead the suit again.

Here is a simpler case, where you have an intermediate card:

♠ Q 7 6

♠ K 10 8

Partner leads the ♠2 against 4♡ and dummy plays the ♠6.

Again, you preserve your king for the killing of dummy's queen, but this time your ♠10 will be a powerful weapon. Since partner will not have the ace (he has already read Tip 55!), you know he has the jack; so your ten will force declarer's ace:

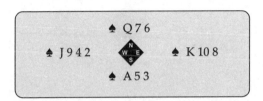

On the second round, partner can lead his jack and your king is ready for dummy's queen.

A last example:

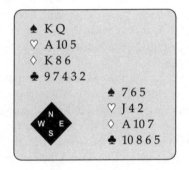

North	South
	1♠
2♣	2♠
3♠	Pass

Your partner leads the ♡3 against 3♠ by South. Dummy plays small. What will happen if you play the jack? Declarer will win with his honour and have a simple finesse against your partner's honour. Keep your jack to kill dummy's ten. Declarer wins the first trick with the ♡6, plays a trump to dummy and leads a club to his king and partner's ace. Partner now leads the ◊2 and dummy follows small. Once again, you keep your honour back – your ace has its sight set on dummy's king. Your ten is captured by declarer's queen and your work is nearly done.

The full deal is:

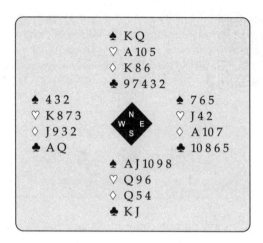

Declarer exits with the ♣J, and partner wins his queen and finishes off the diamond suit by leading the ◊J, squashing dummy's king. After taking your diamond tricks you lead a trump back and declarer can try to establish the club suit, but with the 4-2 break he has to give up. Eventually he has to play hearts himself and give you one more trick – one down.

Notice both your plays in the red suits: a mistake in either one and declarer has an easy ride. The heart suit was especially difficult: your partner did not make a good choice of lead, a trump would have been safer. However, you did well not to compound his error. Can you see that if you put up your jack on the first round, then the queen would take it and your partner's king would be left within the claws of dummy's ace-ten?

It is rare that you should play low on partner's lead, but if you can see that by doing so you protect partner's honour from future danger, you should do so – especially if in the process you preserve your chances of killing an honour in dummy.

Try to show partner your solid honour sequences

Solid sequences are such a blessing: they make leading easy because they are so safe, and they quickly set up tricks. For example, a holding such as ♠K-Q-J-10 is wonderful: a lead of the suit cannot possibly give anything away and at the same time it is likely to establish tricks.

When you make a lead from a solid sequence, always lead the top card: this shows partner you mean business and need very little help from him in the suit. Hence partner will be keen to return it, even when he holds just a few small cards.

Most bridge players know the value of a solid-sequence lead, but perhaps a little rarer is the opportunity to discard a high card to show a solid sequence. You would discard the top of the sequence to show your run, or follow suit with a high card to show your sequence:

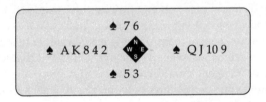

In this situation, when your partner leads the ♠A, you should follow with the ♠Q: this shows that you hold the jack too, and can be invaluable in granting an entry to your hand. On the second round partner can confidently underlead his king and put you in with your jack, to find a killing switch through declarer.

A discard from a top of sequence tends to be very useful when declarer is running a long suit and the two defenders have to decide what to keep; if one defender can show great strength in a suit by showing his sequence, this will make his partner's life a lot easier, allowing him to discard that suit.

Overleaf is an example of such a situation:

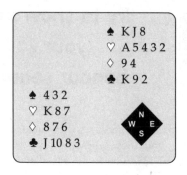

North	South
1♡	4NT
5◊	5NT
6♡	7NT
Pass	

South was determined to punish his partner for opening light! Are you able to punish South for overbidding?

You lead a spade because South is unlikely to have length there; declarer wins it and plays off eight tricks: three spade tricks including the first, and five diamond tricks: ◊A-K-Q-J-10.

What are your last five cards? Having read an earlier tip on discarding (Tip 43), you will want to keep your four clubs, but that would mean baring your ♡K. What should you do?

Fortunately your partner comes to the rescue; his first discard is the ♡Q and now you know what to do:

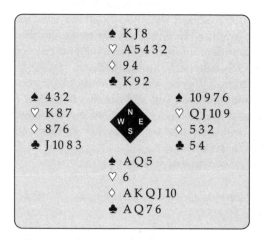

Your partner has very little to think about, but he realises that you will be under a lot of pressure. The ♡Q discard is excellent: it tells you that he has a solid sequence in hearts and he can therefore look after that suit. All your worries are gone; you can happily throw away your hearts and keep the all-important clubs.

This last deal shows how you can help your partner work out what to lead:

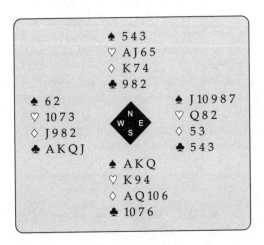

	North	South
		1◊
	1♡	2NT
	3NT	Pass

West led out his four club winners and East discarded the ♠J on the last of them. Can you see how helpful this is to West? Unsure of how to proceed, he would not have been keen on switching to a spade (leading into declarer's strength), but since East has suggested a solid suit West can happily lead a spade – not expecting to make a trick from the suit, but knowing that it is a safe lead.

As you can see, any other switch will allow declarer to make an extra trick in the suit. With a spade switch, declarer cannot succeed; having discarded a heart from his hand on the fourth club, his only options are to look for some luck in diamonds or hearts, neither of which will reward him.

Whenever you are dealt a solid sequence, try to make use of it, ideally by leading the top of it, but following to partner's lead with the top, or discarding the top, can be just as successful measures.

Lead the normal card when leading partner's suit

The most commonly misquoted rule is "Lead top of partner's suit." It is very much a relic from the past and has obviously been taught to many players. However, while there are good reasons for the standard leading methods, there is no reason why leading your partner's suit should be any different.

"But partner needs to know if you have an honour!" shouts someone from the back of the room. "If you lead a low card, then that promises an honour," I reply.

Your honour has a job to do: only lead it if you have a doubleton, when it would be natural to lead top of a doubleton.

Here is a simple example (in no-trumps), where it is your king's job to kill South's queen. Your partner has bid clubs (not unreasonably), but if you lead the ♣K, then South's queen will make a trick. The correct lead of low from three to an honour allows your partner to win his ace and lead the ♣J back.

It is also very important for your partner to be able to judge how many cards you have in his suit. If you always lead the top card then you could have any number, but if you only lead top of a doubleton, then he will be able to judge more accurately:

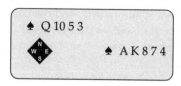

You have bid spades and your partner leads the ♠J, which is covered by

---

Tips for Better Bridge

the queen and your ace; you cash your king knowing that partner has two spades at most (a doubleton or a singleton), and then play a third round allowing partner to ruff (or overruff declarer). Had your partner had three spades, he would not have led ♠J – but a player belonging to the "old school" would have:

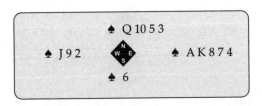

What a disaster that would be! The ♠J is covered by queen and king and then if you try to cash your ace it is ruffed away. The correct lead would, of course, have been the ♠2.

Here is a deal which illustrates yet another reason for not leading the top card:

West	North	East	South
	1♣	1◊	1NT
Pass	3NT	All Pass	

You are on lead against 3NT and you correctly choose the ◊2 as your lead. Your partner wins the ◊A, plays the ♠A and then leads a diamond back to your king. What do you do now?

```
                    ♠ Q 10 5 2
                    ♡ K J 4
                    ◊ 6
                    ♣ A K Q J 5
    ♠ 6 4 3                          ♠ A K J
    ♡ 9 7 6 2          N             ♡ 10 8 5
    ◊ K 3 2         W     E          ◊ A 10 9 7 5
    ♣ 8 3 2            S             ♣ 7 6
                    ♠ 9 8 7
                    ♡ A Q 3
                    ◊ Q J 8 4
                    ♣ 10 9 4
```

Your partner's play of cleverly cashing the ♠A before returning his second diamond should have given you the clue as to what to play: a spade, which allows your partner to take two more spade tricks to defeat 3NT.

Had you led the ◊K you would have needed to work out what to do there and then, for that would have been your last chance: with no other entry, a spade switch is required immediately. If you had managed that, then I think I would like you as my partner!

Knowing what to do at trick one or two is never easy, so by keeping your entry for later you may find yourself faced with a slightly easier decision, thus increasing the likelihood of a successful defence.

I hope I have shown enough reasons to persuade you that leading the top of your partner's suit is not necessarily correct. You should follow your normal leading methods: fourth highest from an honour, top of doubleton, etc., irrespective of whether you are leading your partner's suit or an unbid suit.

If you have A-x-x in your partner's suit and you are on lead against a suit contract, then bear in mind the next tip: you should not lead a small card. In fact you should lead a different suit if at all possible. Only if you feel it is absolutely necessary should you lead the suit, and in that case the best lead would be the ace. However, you should try to avoid leading unsupported aces.

Never underlead an ace at trick one in a suit contract

This rule or tip is probably in every bridge book on your shelf; it really is worth heeding! For partnership harmony I recommend following this rule to the letter, because it can cause great problems if you do underlead an ace and it goes wrong.

By "underleading" I mean leading a small card from a suit in which you hold the ace.

The first and most obvious reason for not underleading an ace is because declarer might have a singleton in the suit and thus your ace will never have a chance to make. But perhaps more importantly, if not quite as drastic, you partner will assume you do not have the ace:

Your partner leads the ♡3 against 4♠, dummy plays the seven and it is your play.

Partner has led a small card, which promises an honour, but he cannot have the ace (he wouldn't underlead it), so he must have the jack and thus you can confidently insert the ten:

The ten forces the ace and the queen is now pincered between jack and king. However, look at the mess that would be caused if partner had underled the ace:

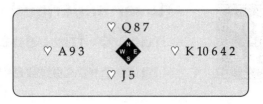

$\heartsuit$ Q 8 7

$\heartsuit$ A 9 3 $\heartsuit$ K 10 6 4 2

$\heartsuit$ J 5

You would quite correctly insert the ten, but now declarer could win his jack and would only lose one trick in the suit (he can ruff the third round).

Later on in the play underleading an ace is certainly allowed, but not on the first lead. Underleading an ace is also fine in no-trump contracts: on the layout above, you would not mind losing the first trick to the jack in a no-trump contract, because you could then take the next four tricks in the suit.

Ideally you should avoid leading a suit with an unsupported ace (i.e. without the king) against a suit contract, but if you have to lead the suit then lead the ace. However, leading an unsupported ace should be a very rare thing to do – after all, the ace's job is to kill an honour.

Here is a lead problem. You are West and the auction is:

	North	South
♠ 4 3 2		1♠
♡ A 7 6	3♠	4♠
♢ A 9 8	All Pass	
♣ A 8 6 5		

What do you lead?

Not a heart, because you can't lead from an ace and you don't want to lead an unsupported ace; not a diamond, because you can't lead from an ace and you don't want to lead an unsupported ace, and of course a club is no good either – thus the only solution is to lead a trump. A trump is by far the best lead from this hand, keeping your aces back to kill honours and making sure they pull their weight!

If you ask a professional whether there is one rule he values above any other, most will quote this one. Yes, perhaps once a year they will break it, but not much more than that.

Be wary of leading from four cards to only one honour

Against no-trump contracts you should tend to lead your longest and strongest suit. When this is a five-card suit, there is a fair chance that you will get something back after taking the risk of leading it: there is hope that your side will establish the suit and you might make two or three extra tricks – you don't mind giving one trick away if you are getting so much back. However, the same is not always true for a four-card suit: taking the same risks can be foolhardy, for you might give a trick away and never get one back, or at least you will only get one back.

When considering a lead from a four-card suit, consider how much you require from your partner to help you; also look at the intermediates: if your second and third cards are strong, you may well make the last two tricks in the suit, so it will be worth it. E.g.

♠ Q 9 8 3   This suit has some merit because the eight and nine might pull their weight.

♡ Q 7 5 2   This suit is very risky: leading away from a queen will quite possibly cost a trick and you have little hope of getting much back.

♢ Q 7 5 3 2   Not a strong suit, but since you have five cards there is some hope that you might make a couple of tricks eventually.

♣ K J 7 3   Not so bad a suit to lead, because you do not need so much from your partner to establish at least two tricks – if not three or four!

The least desirable leads are from four-card suits with just one honour and no intermediates (like the heart suit above). They are especially undesirable at duplicate pairs because they can often give away more than they gain.

When honours are split around the table, a lead from anyone will very often give away one or even two tricks:

♡ A 8 5

♡ K 7 4 3   ♡ J 6 2

♡ Q 10 9

If you lead the ♡3 your partner is likely to put in the jack and declarer will make three tricks in the suit (your king is easily finessed on the second round). You will be lucky if you have enough time to establish your fourth heart, but even that is small compensation.

See how things change when you have two honours:

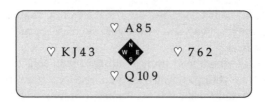

♡ A 8 5

♡ K J 4 3   ♡ 7 6 2

♡ Q 10 9

The ♡3 lead does not look particularly successful, won by dummy's eight, but if partner leads the second round of the suit through declarer's queen you can knock out the ace and make two tricks in the suit.

What else can you lead if your suit is not "desirable"?

Quite often the opponents will have bid two suits before going to no-trumps, so consider one of the unbid suits: it is quite likely that your partner will have some length there and you will be leading towards his honours. With this in mind, what would you lead after the following auction with the hand below?

West	North	East	South
			1♡
Pass	1♠	Pass	2NT[1]
Pass	3NT	All Pass	

[1] 18-19 high-card points

♠ J 5 3 2
♡ 5 4
◇ K 8 4 3
♣ 9 8 6

Your diamond suit is a little ropy and you would do best to steer clear of it. With two unbid suits, if your suit is no good, then try the other; it is quite reasonable to hope that your partner might have something there. Lead the ♣9*.

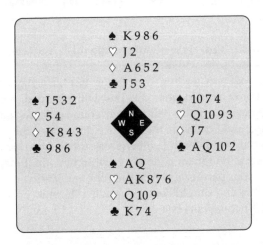

Because you led the nine, partner is able to follow with the two, declarer winning his king and next leading a heart to the jack and East's queen. East now cashes his clubs and exits with the ♡10, leaving declarer with no chance of making nine tricks.

The "normal" diamond lead gives declarer three tricks in the suit: East will contribute the jack, taken by declarer's queen and then your king will be exposed to a finesse. With five top tricks in the major suits and the ♣K destined to score, declarer has his nine tricks already.

Another thing to bear in mind when leading from a weakish suit is that if you do not have much strength outside, the likelihood of being able to make your established suit is very low – not only will you need a lot of help from your partner, but you will also need an entry.

Try to avoid leading four-card suits with just one honour and no intermediates – it tends to give away more than it gains.

*Note that the usual lead from a three-card suit with three small cards is the middle card, MUD style (middle-up-down), but in no-trumps, where distinguishing between doubletons and tripletons is less important, it can be wiser to lead the highest card. It will often help your partner with his play; this is especially true when the two highest cards are touching.

Lead a higher card from a suit without an honour

TIP 57

Your normal lead style should distinguish between suits with honours and suits without.

The most common leading convention is fourth highest from an honour, but you should combine this with "second highest from nothing", playing a higher card when your suit does not have an honour. You should continue this practice throughout the play.

It is important to differentiate between suits headed by an honour and suits that, although long, do not have an honour. It makes a lot of difference to your partner's play at trick one and it also helps your side decide whether you should continue leading the suit.

Look at the two layouts below:

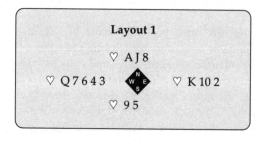

Layout 1

♡ A J 8

♡ Q 7 6 4 3   ♡ K 10 2

♡ 9 5

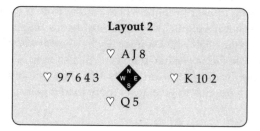

Layout 2

♡ A J 8

♡ 9 7 6 4 3   ♡ K 10 2

♡ Q 5

If your partner leads ♡4 in both layouts, then you will insert the ♡10 when dummy plays low. This works fine in Layout 1 because it wins the trick and you can return the king to knock out the ace, eventually allowing partner's queen to finish off the suit.

However, in Layout 2 your ten loses to the queen. Although things might be OK if your partner gains the lead to play the suit through dummy again, more likely is that a cunning declarer will make sure that he puts *you* on lead next. Now you will be stuck, unable to lead the suit from your side of the table. Had your partner led the ♡7 you could have won your king and led a heart straight back and, if so, either defender could have led the suit without problem. Furthermore, if you can win the ♡K straightaway you can, if you wish, switch to another suit: knowing that partner has no honour in the suit led, you may decide that another suit has better prospects.

Worse still would be the scenario in a suit contract: it is still correct to play the ♡10 (since your partner's low lead promises an honour); what a calamity in Layout 2 when the queen wins the first trick! If declarer does not need a third heart trick, he will win the second trick with the ace, and then your king will be ruffed away! This should demonstrate the need to show or deny an honour with your lead.

When choosing a lead from a "bad" suit, it is standard to lead the second highest, because sometimes it is important to keep the highest card to win the third trick:

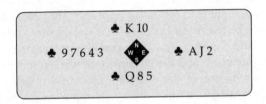

♣ K 10

♣ 9 7 6 4 3   W E   ♣ A J 2

♣ Q 8 5

You lead the ♣7 to the ten, jack and queen; on the next round the ace fells the king and your nine wins the third round. Had you led the nine, then declarer's eight would have won the third round.

Since it is important to differentiate between suits with and without honours throughout the play, you should always lead a higher card when you have no honour, as illustrated by the deal on the next page:

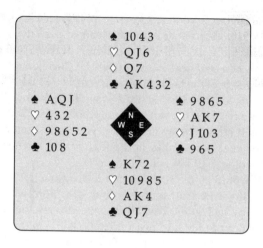

♠ 10 4 3
♡ Q J 6
◇ Q 7
♣ A K 4 3 2

♠ A Q J
♡ 4 3 2
◇ 9 8 6 5 2
♣ 10 8

♠ 9 8 6 5
♡ A K 7
◇ J 10 3
♣ 9 6 5

♠ K 7 2
♡ 10 9 8 5
◇ A K 4
♣ Q J 7

South opens with a 12-14 1NT and North raises directly to 3NT. West chooses to lead a diamond and decides on the ◇8 , denying an honour. Declarer wins the ◇Q and leads the ♡6. East is quite rightly suspicious of this lead, and wins his ♡K.

East's first thought is to return his partner's suit – he obviously has length there – but with no honours, that would mean knocking out both the ace and the king, and there certainly won't be time for that. Best to look elsewhere and there is only one suit left other than clubs, which are clearly out of the question. Having worked out that he should lead a spade, East must choose the right one – a high one – so he plays the ♠8. West wins with the ♠J and, knowing his partner does not have the king (high lead denies an honour), he plays back a heart to partner's ace. Now a second spade lead allows the defence to take their five tricks.

The defence needed both high leads: had West led a low diamond, East would have correctly continued with the suit, hoping partner had the ace or king. Later on, had East switched to a low spade, West would have placed him with the ♠K, and therefore would have won his jack and immediately cashed his ace.

By distinguishing between leads from suits with and without honours you will immensely increase the accuracy of your defence.

Lead through "beatable" strength and up to weakness

If you see a suit with three small cards in dummy it should say one of two things to you, depending on which side of dummy you are seated:

Dummy

♠ 7 6 5

As West you would *not* be keen to lead the suit, because you would be leading up to any strength that declarer had, but as East you would be very keen to lead the suit because you can lead through any strength that declarer has.

Dummy

♡ A Q

By contrast, this time West would be keen to lead a heart – through dummy's strength – hoping to find partner with the king. East, of course, would steer clear of the suit.

These two examples illustrate the general rule: "Lead through strength and up to weakness", i.e. East should be looking for a weak suit in dummy to lead, whilst West should be looking for a strong suit in dummy.

West's hope is that East can kill one of dummy's cards; and East's hope is that West can kill one of declarer's cards.

Dummy

♦ A 7 3 2

Who might want to lead this suit?

This is where it gets a little murkier! West only wants to lead a suit in which East can kill something in dummy; this clearly is not the case here and so West would prefer not to lead a diamond. East is more likely to prefer a lead in the suit, hoping to lead through intermediate strength in declarer's hand. For this reason, I like to qualify "Lead through strength" by adding a word: "Lead through *beatable* strength".

Quite often you will continue with the suit you led in the first place, but when you are holding a weak hand and are likely to only have one entry, then consider switching if a particular suit looks desirable, otherwise your side may never be able to lead the suit profitably:

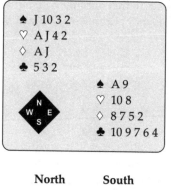

♠ J 10 3 2
♡ A J 4 2
♦ A J
♣ 5 3 2

♠ A 9
♡ 10 8
♦ 8 7 5 2
♣ 10 9 7 6 4

North	South
	1♠
3♠	4♠
Pass	

After a quick auction, your partner leads the ◊K. Declarer wins with his ace and sets about drawing trumps. Do you have a plan?

When you win your ♠A you will get your one and only chance to affect the outcome of the hand. You could lead back a diamond to your partner's queen, but that is not going to be enough: your side will need more. Look at dummy: as East you should be looking for weakness and the clubs stand out by a long way. Your side is going to need a number of club tricks and it is probably important that the first club lead should come from your hand. This will allow you to trap any strength that declarer has underneath partner's strength. Then, when partner gets the lead, he will be able to take his ◇Q himself.

The full deal is:

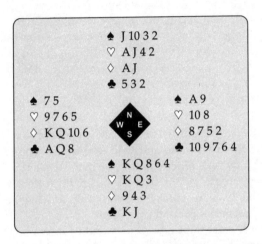

```
              ♠ J 10 3 2
              ♡ A J 4 2
              ◇ A J
              ♣ 5 3 2
  ♠ 7 5                    ♠ A 9
  ♡ 9 7 6 5       N        ♡ 10 8
  ◇ K Q 10 6   W     E     ◇ 8 7 5 2
  ♣ A Q 8         S        ♣ 10 9 7 6 4
              ♠ K Q 8 6 4
              ♡ K Q 3
              ◇ 9 4 3
              ♣ K J
```

As you can see, a club switch allows your side to take four tricks and defeat 4♠ by one trick. If instead you led back a diamond, your partner would have won it, but then he would have been stuck. He could not lead a club without giving a trick to declarer's king but if he did not play a club, declarer could discard one on the heart suit.

Switching to the right suit is a habit worth acquiring. It is especially important when you hold a weak hand which is only likely to gain the lead once: you need to help your partner, and the way to work out how best to do that will often be evident by looking at dummy.

Cash your winners before trying for a trump promotion

Firstly of all let us see how a trump promotion works:

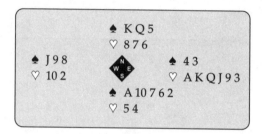

Spades are the trump suit. Your partner leads your suit, hearts, and you take the first two tricks and then lead a third round. What can declarer do? If he ruffs high with the ace, then West's jack will make a trick on the third round of trumps, but if he ruffs low, West can overruff. Either way West makes a trump trick, to which he would not normally be entitled – a trump promotion.

This is a very important type of play and its timing may be crucial, because sometimes declarer will decide not to ruff at all, especially if he has a loser he needs to dispose of anyway. It is best for the defence to try to take their winners before they pursue a trump promotion.

For example:

West	North	East	South
			1♣
Pass	1♡	Pass	1♠
Pass	3♠	Pass	4♠
All Pass			

Your partner leads ♡9, which declarer covers with the queen. How do you defend?

It looks like your opponents have just a 4-4 spade fit, so there is a fair chance that you might be able to promote a trump trick for your partner by continuing hearts. If you win the ♡A-K and play a third heart, you will be disappointed to see declarer discard a diamond. Your partner makes his trump trick, but your diamond trick has gone missing. Look carefully at the full deal:

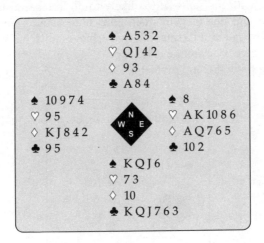

```
              ♠ A 5 3 2
              ♡ Q J 4 2
              ◇ 9 3
              ♣ A 8 4
  ♠ 10 9 7 4           ♠ 8
  ♡ 9 5          N     ♡ A K 10 8 6
  ◇ K J 8 4 2  W   E   ◇ A Q 7 6 5
  ♣ 9 5            S    ♣ 10 2
              ♠ K Q J 6
              ♡ 7 3
              ◇ 10
              ♣ K Q J 7 6 3
```

Before you aim for your trump promotion, you should cash your winners, here the ◇A. Now when you play the third heart declarer is stuck: he has already lost three tricks, but he cannot avoid losing a trump trick. He will be hoping for a normal 3-2 break, so he will ruff high and try to draw trumps, only to find that West's ten will be outstanding.

It is important to look out for opportunities to gain a trump promotion but don't be too eager; consider instead if there are tricks you should be taking first.

Be patient
when defending
against 1NT

In the declarer-play section you will have already read my tip to be patient when playing 1NT. Well, both sides need patience. Tip 34 showed that opening up suits where the honours are divided between the four players is dangerous, and thus if you can force your opponents to play new suits you will tend to gain.

Too often defenders who think they have "missed" with their opening lead will feel the need to go searching elsewhere, whereas continuing with the same suit is likely to do less harm. It might not gain much, but one of your main aims is to avoid giving anything away: you do not mind a safe lead that achieves little, but you do mind a lead that gives declarer an extra trick.

Consider the following problem:

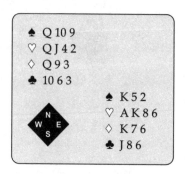

West	North	East	South
			1♣[1]
Pass	1♡	Pass	1NT[2]
All Pass			

[1] May not be natural
[2] 12-14 points

North-South are playing five-card majors and a strong no-trump, so South has shown 12-14 points and will not necessarily have four clubs. Your partner leads the ♠3 to dummy's nine and you need to make a plan now.

You could play small following Tip 47, keeping your king to kill dummy's queen, but what is your plan when you next get the lead?

Both club and diamond leads could be dangerous: remember that the job of your ◇K and ♣J is to kill the ◇Q and the ♣10 respectively: this is something they cannot do if you lead away from them. Since your partner led spades, it is not unreasonable to plan to continue playing on that suit. Bearing this in mind, at trick one you play the ♠K, which loses to declarer's ace. Declarer now continues with a heart to the queen.

Partner certainly didn't strike gold with his lead: unfortunately declarer will make three tricks in spades, but that does not mean you should not continue leading them. As indeed this is the plan you have chosen, you win the ♡K and continue with spades. Do not feel you have given a second trick away by leading into the ♠Q-10: everybody knows where the jack is! The main consideration is that your passive defence may gain a trick in the long run. This is the full deal:

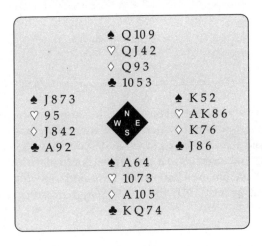

Declarer wins the second spade in dummy and leads another heart to his ten (you duck), and then a third heart. You win this and cash your fourth winning heart. Once again you continue with spades – not giving anything away. Declarer wins the third spade in dummy and leads a club to the king, but your partner ducks this and declarer is stuck: you have forced him to lead away from his hand. A good guess and declarer can get home, but you have made him work very hard and more than likely you will prevail.

The endgame has many permutations, but more important is the fact that both a club and a diamond lead would have given up a trick straight away if you led them early.

It is very easy to panic after what appears to be a calamitous lead and search elsewhere, but any lead would be calamitous on this deal! What is important is to give away tricks in one suit only, rather than in them all.

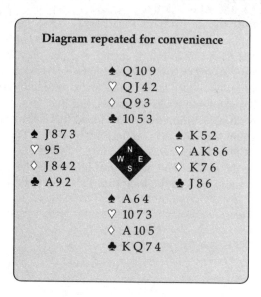

Diagram repeated for convenience

♠ Q 10 9
♡ Q J 4 2
◇ Q 9 3
♣ 10 5 3

♠ J 8 7 3　　　　♠ K 5 2
♡ 9 5　　　　　　♡ A K 8 6
◇ J 8 4 2　　　　◇ K 7 6
♣ A 9 2　　　　　♣ J 8 6

♠ A 6 4
♡ 10 7 3
◇ A 10 5
♣ K Q 7 4

I can quite easily imagine an East switching to a diamond when in with the ♡K; if West puts up his ◇J, then declarer makes three tricks in that suit too! And then the East player, in despair, takes the second heart with his ace and switches to a club. When South plays low, West has to play his ace on thin air – that would leave declarer with ten tricks!

Be patient against 1NT; try not to play new suits without good reason.

Trump leads can be safe throughout the play

In duplicate pairs, the aim of a defender is not so clearly defined as it might be at teams or rubber bridge: you are not simply trying to defeat the contract but you are actually aiming to make as many tricks as you possibly can. You should not take a risky action to try to defeat a contract if that action, should it be unsuccessful, presents declarer with an overtrick. In fact, generally, when defending at pairs you should take as few risks as possible: let declarer go wrong and give him no help. To this end, trump leads can be very useful, not only at your first turn, but throughout the play. It means that you do not have to open up a new suit – you can just leave the hard work up to declarer.

For example:

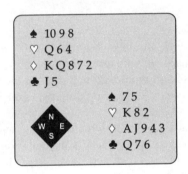

	♠ 10 9 8
	♡ Q 6 4
	◇ K Q 8 7 2
	♣ J 5

		♠ 7 5
	N	♡ K 8 2
W	E	◇ A J 9 4 3
	S	♣ Q 7 6

West	North	East	South
			1♠
Pass	2♠	Pass	4♠
All Pass			

Your partner leads a trump against 4♠. Declarer wins in hand and leads the ◇10 to dummy's king. Plan your defence.

Are you thinking that a club switch may be promising, through declarer's supposed strength?

Be careful: hearts and clubs might look like good switches – because of the supposed weakness in dummy – but your honours want to kill the honours in dummy and they can't do that if you lead away from them. Declarer is surely going to struggle since it seems he is trying to establish his diamond suit when you, of course, know that the suit is breaking nastily. Let declarer struggle and he will probably have to play hearts and clubs himself – play a "safe" trump back.

Now look at the full deal:

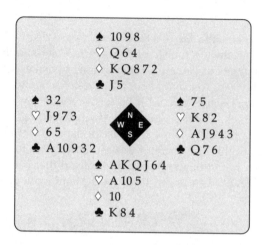

```
                    ♠ 10 9 8
                    ♡ Q 6 4
                    ◊ K Q 8 7 2
                    ♣ J 5
      ♠ 3 2              N          ♠ 7 5
      ♡ J 9 7 3      W       E      ♡ K 8 2
      ◊ 6 5              S          ◊ A J 9 4 3
      ♣ A 10 9 3 2                  ♣ Q 7 6
                    ♠ A K Q J 6 4
                    ♡ A 10 5
                    ◊ 10
                    ♣ K 8 4
```

A club or heart switch would give a trick away – a club forces your partner to play his ace on "thin air" to win the trick, after declarer has played low; and a heart would allow dummy's queen to make. Even a diamond would be costly, allowing dummy's ◊8-7 to come into their own.

However, you have chosen to return a trump and now declarer is stuck, having to play clubs and hearts himself. Note that if declarer plays the heart suit himself then your king can kill his queen and your partner's jack takes care of the ten, leaving declarer with just one trick in the suit. The story is similar in clubs: the defenders' honours can kill declarer's honours. There is no doubt that the trump return has done its job, keeping your honours in the side-suits safe.

When playing duplicate pairs, if faced with a choice of plays, choose the safe option unless there is a need for urgency. One of the safest leads in the middle game is a trump.

GENERAL TIPS

Do not put important cards at either end of your hand

Have you ever seen anybody's cards when you're playing bridge? I know I have – my first action is to ask my opponents to hold their cards higher. It is very difficult when they are flashing their cards at you, especially when you see a high card which is almost inevitably going to have a huge bearing on the play.

I am sure my cards have been seen by my opponents too, but one tactic I was taught a long time ago is to avoid having your high cards on the edges of your hand. It might seem a little odd, because you like to have your cards in order but if you possibly can, try to put twos and threes on the edge. Then, when your opponents catch a glimpse of a card, what they will see will not affect the play at all.

Better than moving your high cards from the ends is to make sure you hold your cards higher in the first place. It is an error that too many bridge players are guilty of and it is important to understand that although you might be giving your opponents an advantage you are also putting them under ethical pressure. They do not want to see your cards!

Another thing to bear in mind when arranging your cards in your hand is that you should avoid always placing the cards in the right order. Some clever opponents might notice you taking cards from here and there, and work out your holdings when you play you lowest and highest cards. The easiest way to overcome this is to keep them in order for the bidding, so that you can easily evaluate your hand, but perhaps displace a few cards for the play – especially a few lower ones which you could place at either end!

Simple tactics like these can make a lot of difference to your bridge scores: if your opponents don't know where the aces are, they are going to find their life a lot more difficult!

TIP 63

Avoid
being declarer
when you are dummy

This is probably the most important tip: if you can become a better dummy, you will be amazed at how much your bridge will progress; your partnership will be better as a whole, but you will also have more energy for the rest of your game.

It certainly took me a long time; I used to keep a close eye on my partner's play, ready to pounce on any mistake – to what end?

Your partner is not going to enjoy your comments, nor are your opponents. Bridge is a partnership game; your aim should be to promote partnership harmony, so trust your partner to play the cards and relax while he does so and conserve your energy for your future decisions.

The things that dummy can do are limited:

1. Dummy is allowed to prevent an irregularity occurring, but he is not able to point it out once it has occurred (until the play is over).
2. Dummy is allowed to ask partner whether he has any of a suit remaining, when he discards on an opponent's (or dummy's) lead.
3. Dummy can keep track of the number of tricks lost or won.

Dummy is, as the name suggests, a relatively redundant personage but this must not be an invitation to get active and study the cards your partner is playing. Bridge is a complex and fascinating game and there is always so much to think about, so use your time as dummy to relax and get ready for the next burst of thought required. When you play the next deal you will be glad of not having to think about partner's mistakes or brilliancies, instead you will have a clearer head, ready to find the perfect line.

The number of times that dummy will make a comment detrimental to his partner at the end of play is extraordinary. Go to the bar and get your partner a drink – he will certainly appreciate that a lot more.

Before you lead ask for a review of the auction

When your opponents alert, you are allowed (at your turn to call) to ask the partner of the bidder what the alerted bid means. I only recommend doing this when you really need to know: obviously if you have a good hand and want to bid, the information is important, but when you are not thinking of bidding, the time you need to know is when you are about to lead: at the end of the auction. There are three reasons for delaying your questions:

1. By asking you might be compromising yourself. Your questioning could be construed as suggesting that you have some interest in the auction and thus your partner might be under a little ethical pressure not to take advantage.
2. If the opponents are in the middle of a slightly complex auction, they will have to tell you all the relays and responses, whereas at the end of the auction they can explain in summary.

West	East
1♣	1♡
1NT	3NT
All Pass	

The 1♣ opening bid was alerted because it could be any number of different hands: 12-14 balanced, or 16+ any shape; or natural with clubs.

Do you really want to hear all of this? It is confusing, is it not?

By the end of the auction, when it is your turn to lead, you ask what the bidding means and you are told that West has shown 12-14 points with a balanced hand; he should have three or more clubs. Now on the basis of that simple description you can choose your lead.

3. Perhaps most importantly, your questioning may well bring to light a misunderstanding in the opponents' auction. Although this should not affect their bidding it almost invariably does and allows them to escape from their predicament. It is much better to ask at the end: then, when they discover their misunderstanding, it is too late for them to go back!

TIP 65

Enjoy the game!

This is a very simple tip to finish with, but I think it is one of the most important by far. It is possible to compete to one's best ability and also to enjoy the game at the same time. More important is to make sure your opponents are enjoying themselves too. Obviously when you get a top board, the opponents are going to get a bottom – and there is nothing that can be done to change that!

However, there are many things we can do to make bridge a better and more enjoyable game. Here is a list that paraphrases the top ten "gestures" recommended by the American Contract Bridge League Goodwill Committee:

- Greet and welcome opponents.
- Say: "Thank you, partner."
- Lead or put down dummy before you write the contract in your score-card.
- Help new players progress in the game.
- Always call for the director quietly and politely.
- Compliment opponents' play.
- Discuss hands after the whole game is finished.
- Accept defeat and victory with grace.
- Leave a tidy table.
- Smile often!

Wouldn't it be wonderful if bridge could be always like that? Keep enjoying the game and help others to enjoy it too!